A PSYCHOANALYST
ON HIS OWN COUCH

A PSYCHOANALYST ON HIS OWN COUCH

A Biography of Vamık Volkan and His Psychoanalytic and Psychopolitical Concepts

Ferhat Atik

PHOENIX
PUBLISHING HOUSE
firing the mind

First published in 2019 by
Phoenix Publishing House Ltd
62 Bucknell Road
Bicester
Oxfordshire OX26 2DS

British Library Cataloguing in Publication Data

A C.I.P. for this book is available from the British Library

ISBN-13: 978-1-912691-15-9

Typeset by Medlar Publishing Solutions Pvt Ltd, India

Printed in the United Kingdom

www.firingthemind.com

This book is dedicated to people who experience trauma and who try to address this terrible thing within themselves, perhaps with their inner dynamics and who, hopefully, realize that there really is help out there.

Contents

Foreword

Vamık D. Volkan

Ferhat Atik, the author of this book, had lived through decades-long deadly ethnic conflict on his Mediterranean island, Cyprus. In the mid-2010s, when his environment no longer was dangerous, he came up with an interesting project. He interviewed Cypriot Turks whom he considered public figures, and recorded their predictions about what would happen in the following two and half decades to Turkish Cypriots and their Turkish Republic of Northern Cyprus which had not been recognized internationally. Atik would not share the opinions he collected; the interview videos would be locked in a safe place at his university to be opened twenty-five years later.

Like Atik, I was born to Turkish parents at an earlier time on Cyprus when the island was a British colony. I didn't leave the island until I finished high school and went to Turkey for my medical education. As a newly graduated physician I came to the United States with only fifteen dollars in my pocket and my violin, but I had a job as a medical intern. A few years later I became an American citizen. In the United States I studied psychiatry and psychoanalysis, and starting in the early 1960s I had a faculty position at the University of Virginia's School of Medicine, which I kept for thirty-eight years until my retirement.

In the 1970s a man whom I had never met, President Anwar Sadat of Egypt, opened a new door for me in international relations and large-group psychology. On November 19, 1977, Sadat visited Israel and at the Knesset he spoke about a wall—a psychological barrier—between Egypt and Israel. At that time I was a new member of the American Psychiatric Association's Committee on Psychiatry and Foreign Affairs. The committee assumed the responsibility to study this "wall" by bringing together influential Israelis and Egyptians and, three years later, Palestinians, for six years of unofficial diplomatic dialogues. After the committee's work ended, I continued my work in the international arena alongside my responsibilities as a teacher and administrator at my medical school.

After my retirement, my wife and I began spending our summer months in our home in North Cyprus. I met Atik for the first time in 2013 when he interviewed me for his project mentioned above. I had just finished writing *Enemies on the Couch: A Psychopolitical Journey Through War and Peace*, in which I documented my decades-long work in many conflict-ridden areas of the world, meeting diplomats, political leaders, scholars, children, refugees, and terrorists, and observing historical events such as the collapse of the Soviet Union, the fall of the Berlin Wall, and the tragedy of September 11, 2001 from a psychological angle (Volkan, 2013). Atik took me to a historical location in Famagusta, on the eastern coast of Cyprus, to record my interview.

While we were driving back to my house he wondered what events in my life had led me to spend so much time in places like Israel, Egypt, the Soviet Union, the Baltic republics, the Republic of Georgia, South Ossetia, the former Yugoslavia, Turkey, and Greece, and traumatized societies such as Romania and Albania following the deaths of Nicolae Ceaușescu and Enver Hoxha, respectively, and Kuwait after the invasion by Saddam Hussein's forces was over. He wanted to know why I wanted to examine why human beings—as large groups—fight, humiliate, and kill one another, and what the obstacles are to a peaceful coexistence. He asked me if my being from Cyprus and the ethnic conflict on the island motivated me for working for a peaceful world. He asked if he could visit and talk with me more deeply about these complex questions. I agreed, and this is how Atik's book started.

He met with me in the garden of our Cyprus home three or four times a week during the summers of 2013 and 2014. We joked about my being put on a psychoanalytic couch, talking about my life and describing my professional activities. Then an interesting question came up: Why did I choose to carry out clinical research on mourning when I became a faculty member of the University of Virginia's Medical School? When I began studying the variations of people's responses to losses, I was not aware that I was going through a complicated mourning myself as a traumatized immigrant. I became aware of this fact prior to my conversations with Atik. A traumatic loss that occurs in a person's adult life may unconsciously inflame the mental image of a childhood loss. When I began talking with Atik, one of the first stories I told him was about losing my cat Rengin when I was a child.

My understanding about unconscious motivations behind other professional activities emerged for the first time while I was talking with Atik. For example, I was aware that spending seven years studying the life of Kemal Atatürk, the founder of the Turkish Republic, and writing his psychobiography with Princeton University historian Norman Itzkowitz (Volkan & Itzkowitz, 1984), had a great deal to do with my re-examining my relationship with my father. While talking with Atik I realized a previously unconscious motivation involved in this activity that took place during my initial years in the United States. During those seven years I was reviewing my image of "Turkishness" that I had left behind by coming to the United States. In a sense, I was mourning. Then I kept this image and held onto it while developing my biculturalism as an immigrant. Getting together with Atik was like being on a psychoanalytic couch!

Atik started to read many of my books. After the summer of 2014, every time I was on the island we would meet frequently and I would answer his questions about psychoanalytic concepts by providing detailed examples. He already had begun writing my biography, but his book slowly evolved to include a comprehensive description of my clinical and psychopolitical findings as well, as a kind of textbook.

I am grateful for Atik's skill and interest in communicating my personal life story, intertwined with clear illustrations of my clinical and psychopolitical concepts. And I am grateful for the time spent on his "couch."

About the author

Ferhat Atik is a Turkish Cypriot writer, scriptwriter, and director. Having lectured on economics, media, literature, and cinema at doctorate level, and having published articles in newspapers and journals, Ferhat Atik then became a producer and TV and radio host. He has published many articles, several novels, and various film scripts.

Silk Road, Autumn, Toy Car, Double Port, When There Is Still Time, Kingdom of Lambousa, and *After Tomorrow* are among his published works. Ferhat Atik has directed and written screenplays for short films which have appeared in international film festivals, particularly in Italy, India, and the Far East. His full-length feature film *The Key*, based on his own novel *Autumn*, premiered in the 48th International Antalya Golden Orange Film Festival and was then shown at the 31st Istanbul Film Festival in 2012. Ferhat Atik teaches creative writing and screenwriting at Girne American University in Kyrenia and he is the holder of the 2018 Golden Pen of Freedom, an international press freedom award.

About Vamık Volkan

Dr. Vamık Djemal Volkan was born to Turkish parents in Cyprus in 1932. Before coming to the United States in 1957 he received his medical training at the School of Medicine, University of Ankara, Turkey.

He is emeritus professor of psychiatry at the University of Virginia's School of Medicine in Charlottesville, Virginia. He is also an emeritus training and supervising analyst at the Washington Psychoanalytic Institute in Washington, DC and emeritus senior Erik Erikson Scholar at the Austen Riggs Center, Stockbridge, MA.

Dr. Volkan was one-time medical director of the Blue Ridge Hospital of Virginia University and held the chairmanship of the Center for the Study of Mind and Human Interaction (CSMHI). Dr. Volkan is also among the founders and a former president of the Turkish American Neuropsychiatric Association and the International Society for Political Psychology (ISPP), along with being the former president of the American College of Psychoanalysts. He was an inaugural Yitzhak Rabin Fellow at the Yitzhak Rabin Center in Israel, a visiting professor of law at Harvard University, a visiting professor of political science at the University of Vienna, and a visiting professor of political psychology at Bahçeşehir University in Turkey. He has also served as a visiting professor of psychiatry at Ege University, Ankara University, and Cerrahpaşa University, all in Turkey.

In 1980, with his multidisciplinary team, Vamık launched an initiative to bring together representatives of large groups in conflict for a series of unofficial diplomatic dialogues in order to seek common ground and peaceful coexistence. Speaking with many world leaders and working in refugee camps and visiting Israel, Egypt, the Soviet Union and later Russia, the Baltic Republics, Croatia, Albania, Romania, Kuwait, Georgia, South Ossetia, Turkey, and Greece, over more than three decades, he developed new theories on large-group psychology and suggested new strategies for peaceful coexistence.

Vamık Volkan has been a member of the International Negotiation Network (INN), an organization chaired by former US president Jimmy Carter throughout the 1980s and 1990s. He was a temporary consultant at the World Health Organization (WHO) in Albania and Macedonia. He held the title of Fulbright/Sigmund Freud Foundation Visiting Scholar of Psychoanalysis in Vienna, Austria in 2006. Dr. Volkan has published nearly fifty books and he has contributed to many publications of others as coauthor, editor, and coeditor, and he has penned hundreds of articles. He has been nominated for many awards by numerous organizations around the world and has sat on the executive boards of sixteen journals. Vamık Volkan was nominated for the Nobel Peace Prize five times in the mid-2000s and in 2014, with letters of support coming in from twenty-seven countries.

In 2008, Dr. Volkan founded the International Dialogue Initiative (IDI), becoming its first president. The IDI consists of unofficial representatives from Germany, Iran, Israel, Russia, Turkey, the United Kingdom, the United States, and the West Bank. They meet twice a year to examine world affairs, primarily from a psychopolitical point of view.

About this book

Vamık Volkan, to use his own expression, "puts himself on his own couch," and tells his life story as a psychoanalyst who has seen and studied humans in many parts of the world. Within this book are many concepts Dr. Volkan has introduced into the world that have gained wide acceptance and which have been highly influential.

Because a book about Vamık Volkan is destined not to be a mere biography but also a professional guide, the life of a professor and his real-life stories, a means towards understanding humanity, societies, memories, and modes of psychological treatment, the issue of writing methodology inevitably arises. For this reason, starting in 2013, I interviewed him for hours, sometimes for days and months. In parallel with the interviews, I read the forty-two books that Dr. Volkan had written down the years and I scrutinized them very closely. When I felt I had sufficiently mastered the overall meaning and the minutiae of Dr. Volkan's works, the interviews were transcribed and they became the backbone of the present book.

The words in this biography are, of course, largely mine—it is no autobiography. Yet, I quote extensively from Vamık Volkan's works and utterances. Let it be noted that, at certain points in the book, some of the names, places, and times have been altered in the interests of doctor–patient confidentiality. The scientific terminology employed here has been rigorously checked with Dr. Volkan.

Starting to write a new book is as exciting for me as starting a new life, yet with all the experiences of the past embodied in the work. And this publication is, perhaps, the most absorbing and fulfilling of my writing career to date. One pleasant reflection is that I got the idea of writing Vamık Volkan's biography when driving from Famagusta (a city on the eastern coast of Cyprus), down the breathtaking mountain range that crisscrosses the North, to the delightful town of Kyrenia on the northern littoral. This is where Vamık Volkan has his Cyprus residence and where he spends his summer months.

Starting off was largely a matter of having long conversations with Vamık Volkan, enjoying his hospitality, his courtesy, and his perspectives as a compassionate citizen of the world. Emotional it certainly was and the sense of suffering humanity was always there. As was fun and as was anger; as was grief. I sat attending not just to his words, but also to his tone of voice, his body language, and his rather subtle way of interacting.

Writing a biography has a great deal to do with empathy. As Atticus says in *To Kill a Mockingbird* (Lee, 1961), in order to understand somebody and their concerns, one has to climb into their skin and walk around in it for a while. I believe I have managed to do something like this with Vamık Volkan, due in no small part to the fact that my understanding has arisen largely though Dr. Volkan's firsthand accounts. Hopefully, this will mean a certain sense of immediacy for you, the reader.

A history of Cyprus

Vamık Volkan's story is also the story of Cyprus, so let me tell you something of the island and its rather checkered history.

Cyprus has been named and renamed many times down the centuries and this fact reflects the numerous civilizations which have come and gone. Some are still with us, such as the Greek, the Turkish, the British, the Armenians, and the Jews. For the name of the island, in Turkish we use *Kıbrıs*; in Arabic it is *Kubrus*; she is also known as *Cypre, Kipros, Chypre, Cypern, Cipro, Kipr, Zypern,* and *Cyprus* in various Western languages. Perhaps the oldest documented names are Hittite and Egyptian—*Alaşya, Alasia, Alashia, Asi.* The first time a name close to the present ones was employed was in the works of Homer. This name was *Kypros.* It means copper. For the simple reason that Cyprus was the ancient world's number one source of this very desirable metal and this, to its inhabitants' constant distress, made the island very desirable to invaders.

Looking at various types of archaeological evidence, we can see that the very first humans on the island arrived around 10,000 years before the birth of Christ. As the centuries went by, invaders and traders with an interest in Cyprus multiplied, before gradually fading away one by one.

In ancient times, Cyprus, as Greece, was not one polity but several. The distinct city states were governed locally and interacted with varying degrees of hostility and cooperation. Cyprus stood between the two most dominant

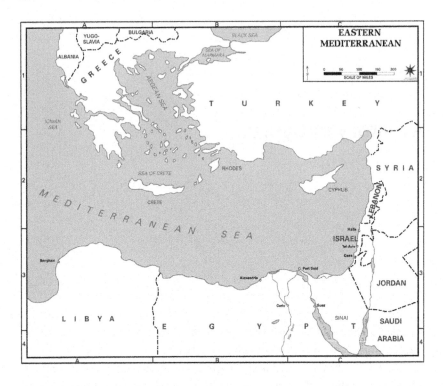

powers of the Bronze Age in the Near and Middle East—the Egyptians and the Hittites. A certain Hittite ruler Tudhaliya III conquered the island in 1320 BC in defiance of the Egyptians and Cyprus became a Hittite colony for 120 years. The Hittites disappeared from the face of the earth in the twelfth century BC and the Egyptians stepped in again.

A new era was being ushered in at this time and the Achaeans and the Dorians, initially nomadic tribes from the North, arrived in the area. These peoples raided and pillaged what we now call the Greek peninsula and gradually settled and became the Mycenaean civilization. They spread across the eastern Mediterranean, to Crete and Rhodes and made inroads into Asia Minor. On arrival in Cyprus, they settled in a way which made the island not a far-flung colony for them but a homeland.

Another set of eyes now fixed on Cyprus as the Phoenicians turned their attention from their insufficiently fertile lands to this desirable island and established sophisticated settlements. They were ousted by the Assyrians, who then winked out, and the ever-persistent Egyptians returned. They fell off their Cypriot perch once again when the

Persian King Cambyses took their motherland in 525 BC, upon which Egyptian possessions fell automatically to the occupying power.

This situation did not last long. An ambitious Macedonian changed the entire course of history in the Near and Middle East, as well as further afield. At the tender age of sixteen, Alexander assumed the kingship after his father had been murdered and, goaded by Aristotle, he undertook the invasion of Asia Minor and the destruction of the Persian Empire. He did not come to Cyprus, but he certainly made her part of his overall plan for the known world. After Alexander's untimely death, one of his generals, Ptolemy, took Cyprus under his control. A state of affairs that lasted until 58 BC.

The Romans arrived as part of their equally Alexandrian need to expand into new regions and Cyprus became a Roman colony. One can be forgiven for thinking that the Roman Empire ceased to exist in AD 471, when Alaric and the Goths took Rome, but this is not so. The Eastern Roman Empire lasted a further thousand years, albeit known as the Byzantine Empire. This empire had among its possessions the small but significant colony of Cyprus. Cyprus under the Byzantine Empire adopted the Greek language and the Greek Orthodox version of Christianity. Cyprus became Orthodox by default.

Islam came to the island little by little. As the Muslim religion was born and started to spread, it came into conflict with the Byzantine Empire. The Arab armies attacked the marches with little success and while coveting the Byzantine possession of Cyprus, twenty-four attempted invasions met with no real success.

When the Third Crusade took its lamentable course, Cyprus changed hands again. Richard I of England took control of the island in 1191 and subsequently sold it to the Knights Templar. It is unlikely he consulted the islanders on the subject of this transaction, who rioted the following year; it seems the Templar administration did not agree with them, and Cyprus was handed back to Richard. He in turn flogged it to the French Lusignan dynasty, which enjoyed a longer period of rule. Guy de Lusignan was ejected from Jerusalem, where he had purported to be king, so he switched his kingdom to Cyprus. The Lusignan era yielded twelve kings.

The Lusignan period saw a rise in the general welfare of the people and great architectural works were undertaken, many of which can still be seen today. With Cyprus being a crusader base, and with her strategic position seen as blocking shipping from Anatolia, the Mamluks (a dynasty controlling Egypt, the Hejaz, and parts of the Levant) attacked the island. They occupied it in 1426, albeit briefly. They very reasonably allowed the

Lusignans to stay in charge in return for a tribute and withdrew. Yet they continued to interfere in the internal affairs of the island until the Ottoman Turks invaded and took charge more conclusively.

The Ottoman period

When the Ottoman Sultan Selim I conquered Egypt, it was an attempt at exerting hegemony of the Mediterranean region. To facilitate this, Cyprus was key. Furthermore, Orthodox Christians on the island who were compelled to be Catholics, people groaning under heavy taxation, and the disgruntled in general sent delegations to Istanbul/Constantinople to seek an Ottoman intervention and their words did not fall on deaf ears. With the relative strength of the Turks, once the decision had been taken to invade Cyprus, the outcome was in little doubt. The invasion began on July 2, 1570. The acquisition of the island was completed on August 1.

Once the Ottomans had conquered the island, Cyprus was turned administratively into a *beylerbeylik* (province) with Nicosia as its center. Settlement followed and a decree dated September 22, 1572 facilitated large-scale migration to the island. In total 1,689 families were earmarked to be sent to Cyprus. The population of Cyprus increased. Cypriot Greeks, anxious about their lives, their property, and their honor during the Venetian Period, found themselves in a situation of peace and security and, most important, parting with half the tax they previously paid.

The Ottoman Empire left important traces on the island. The rule of three centuries transformed the island, very importantly, in terms of law. Compulsory unpaid labor among the community in general ended and religious tolerance arrived. The Orthodox archbishop was recalled, having languished in exile. Invasion it may have been, but it ushered in a liberal period.

The Ottoman Empire allowed not only its own subjects, that is, the people it transferred, but the entire island population to live more or less freely and develop their economies and cultures throughout the 308 years they held sway.

Leasing the island to the United Kingdom

British interest in Cyprus was doubtless stimulated by the Crimean War. The lead-up to this rather strange conflict started when the governor of Egypt, Muhammad Ali, repudiated Ottoman rule and went for independence.

Russia, which had long coveted Istanbul/Constantinople, and had also long desired a warm water port or two, sniffed an opportunity and it became national policy to destroy the Ottoman Empire. A pretext was needed and one was quickly found in the issue of who was custodian of the sacred sites of the Holy Land. Although the Ottomans granted privileges to the Catholics and the Orthodox Christians in and around Jerusalem, Russia declared that she should have control of these sacred places. For by no means the first time, Russia prepared for war in the name of Jesus the pacifist. In 1853 Russia came into conflict with France, a largely Catholic country and Great Britain, a largely Protestant country. It is likely that their religious differences were shabby excuses. When Russia invaded Romania in that year, Great Britain and France sent forces to the Black Sea region in order to check Russian expansionism, protect trade routes, and prop up the Ottoman Empire—a buffer against the Czar taking control of parts of the Mediterranean. Counting on British and French support, the Turks rejected Russian demands.

History once again called this little island of the Mediterranean onto the stage. The Ottomans declined to sign various protocols, thus gradually losing the support of European powers, and Russia decided to take advantage of their isolation to renew her incursions. On April 24, 1877 she declared war. This time there was no British or French task force to come to the rescue and at San Stefano, on March 3, 1878, a highly punitive treaty was forced on the Turks involving the ceding of large areas of land. Feeling the Bear coming ever closer to her Mediterranean interests, Great Britain approached Turkey with a suggestion for an alliance. On May 25, 1878, the negotiations began. At first the British asked for a base in Anatolia. This would be logical in attempts to oppose Russian expansion—much closer to the potential theatre of operations than her possession, Malta. Then the British plumped for Cyprus. This made sense to a naval power. Sultan Abdul Hamid II was persuaded after a secret meeting to transfer Cyprus to Great Britain on a temporary basis, on the condition that the British would pay 100,000 pounds per annum for the privilege (Simmons, 2015). On June 4, 1878, an agreement was signed under which administration of the island would fall to the British, but which in no way waived Ottoman property rights or overall sovereignty in relation to Cyprus. Thus, 308 years of Ottoman administration came to an end and Abdul Hamid issued a decree on July 12 of that year as a kind of royal assent. The British side of the bargain was ill-kept and, as things turned out, the property rights and sovereignty issues agreed on were not honored and the UK stayed in full possession of the island until the independent Republic of Cyprus was declared on August 16, 1960.

The British period in Cyprus

With the departure of the Ottoman authorities, many Cypriot Greeks saw a chance to unite with Greece—what is termed *Enosis*. Needless to say, this was by no means what the UK government had in mind and it never happened. But trouble was brewing as very different ideas of what the future should hold formed in the two main communities in the island. The Orthodox archbishop of Cyprus welcomed the incoming British high commissioner with the demand that Britain give the island to Greece, as she had done in the case of the Aegean Islands.

Although these Greek Cypriot demands were doubtless disagreeable to the British, the new decision makers favored the Christian Greeks over the Muslim Turks. Employment was allocated very much to the Greek speakers' benefit and Cypriot Turks were often laid off in the name of "reorganization." This was probably a policy of appeasement, with the idea that if the Greek part of the community were given certain advantages they would pipe down about *Enosis*. If this was the policy, it most certainly did not work and the groundswell for *Enosis* grew—eventually to the point of extreme violence.

Economically deprived Cypriot Turks started to leave the island. Many settled in Anatolia, particularly when the Turkish Republic was established in 1923. The demographics shifted considerably, with the weighting going the Greek way. Moreover, when the Ottoman Empire entered the Great War on the side of the Central Powers, the UK annexed Cyprus and some estimated 8,000 Turkish families who did not want to be British subjects left for Turkey.

The Central Powers, of course, lost the war, but the Turks won the War of Deliverance (as it is known in Turkey) and drove out various occupiers. However, at the Treaty of Lausanne, which settled many affairs after a period of great conflict, Turkey conceded that Cyprus was a British possession and waived any rights to property or administration on the island that might have been seen as inherited from Ottoman times. Cypriot Turks were given a limited time to opt for Turkish citizenship and to relocate to Turkey if British rule did not agree with them.

As mentioned before, the demand for *Enosis* did not wither under economic blandishments. This political desire was deep-rooted. When Winston Churchill, then secretary of state for the colonies, came to Cyprus in 1907 he was handed a document voicing this demand. By 1925 the strident voice gave way to violence with riots and terrorism blighting civic life. During this period of unrest, the British and the Cypriot Greeks fell out rather badly. When, in 1931, there was a revision of tax arrangements, this became an excuse to rise up in what became known as the Octobriana Rebellion, starting on October 21. This could only be put down by bringing reinforcements from Egypt. By then the rebels had set the governor's residence alight.

True to form, the UK offered Cyprus to Greece on the condition that Greece enter the Second World War on the Allied side. Perhaps the Greeks remembered the very similar territorial promises made to the Italians to get them into the First World War, which were not kept. Anyway, they declined.

Greece, in any event, had no choice in the matter of joining WWII, as Fascist Italy most comically invaded from neighboring Albania. They were repelled and chased back deep into Albania by the greatly outnumbered Greek army. Hitler had to pull Mussolini out of the fire, which he did convincingly by sending panzer spearheads and infantry to Greece with highly effective Luftwaffe air cover. Greece fell, the quixotic Churchill pulled British forces out, and any idea of a union between Cyprus and Greece was a dead letter.

In the grim postwar years, Cypriot Greeks were still agitating for *Enosis*. Greece was in a state of civil war, characterized by death marches and mass executions.

Between January 15 and 20, 1950 the Greek Orthodox Church conducted a "plebiscite" on the issue of whether Cyprus should be annexed by Greece. Needless to say, this was no real plebiscite, as only the Greek-speaking part of the population was involved. Also, the political legitimacy of the Church was questionable. The British authorities very reasonably refused to accept the results and a sullen anger resulted. Then in 1955 there was an eruption of fury and violence, when the Cypriot Greeks realized they would not achieve *Enosis* through peaceful means. They did not, however, anticipate that neither would they achieve it through violence.

Cypriot Greeks established an organization called *Ethniki Organosis Kyprion Agoniston* (National Organization of Cypriot Fighters with the acronym EOKA). Guerrillas had already been trained in the Troodos Mountains and the stage was set for an anti-colonial struggle with the unusual, missing ingredient of a desire for independence. Many might have thrown up their hands in horror at the suggestion that EOKA was a terrorist organization, but that is what it was. Its aim was to kill British and Turkish people and that is what it did.

The leader of this organization was Georgios Grivas. Born the fourth child of Theodoros Grivas and Kalomira Hadjimichael in Trikomo on March 22, 1897, Grivas proved himself to be a difficult child. He absconded from home when his father tried to get him to be a doctor and enrolled in the military academy in Athens and became a Greek citizen. He subsequently completed his martial training at the *École Militaire* in Paris. He participated in the Greek invasion of Anatolia and experienced the Greek army's rout and precipitate evacuation. Rising in rank, Grivas found himself chief of staff of Greece's Second Division and must have enjoyed the trouncing of the Italian invasion mentioned above. When the Germans took Greece in their accustomed *Blitzkrieg* manner, he ran a minor resistance organization. After WWII, Grivas tried unsuccessfully to enter politics, then turned his attention to his homeland, vowing to rid it of the British. Incidentally, the UK had just liberated Greece, asking for nothing in return "but their respect." The method proposed for ejecting the British from Cyprus was fairly simple on one level—murder. And this is what Grivas turned his hand to. With the *nom de guerre* Digenis, after a Byzantine legendary hero, he returned to plague the island.

British efforts to put the EOKA insurrection down were fairly patchy. Anthony Eden announced that Cyprus could "never" be independent. This pulled the rug from under moderate Cypriot Greeks who wished for a more flexible negotiating stance and a less shooting-people-and-blowing-them-up stance. The war was on.

As already noted, the Cypriot Turks had no desire to let the Cypriot Greeks drag them into Greece and from 1957 on, covert efforts were made to resist. On August 1, 1958, the Turkish Resistance Organization of Cyprus (TMT) was established with the express intention of preventing *Enosis*.

With Eden's having ruled out independence, there was nevertheless a possibility of some form of home rule and Governor Harding approached Greek Cypriot leaders with this in mind. Here enters Michael Christodoulou, known more widely as Archbishop Makarios III. Born on August 13, 1913 to a poor family—his father was a shepherd—this prodigy became a novice in the Kykkos Monastery near his native Paphos. His less theological secondary education was completed at the Pancyprian Gymnasium in Nicosia, after which he, like Grivas, endured German occupation in Greece as he studied theology and law at the University of Athens, graduating in 1942. When he returned to Cyprus, he became an Orthodox priest, then, on a scholarship, went to Boston University to further his theological studies. While still in Massachusetts, he was elected Bishop of Kition (a small town on the south coast of Cyprus) and he duly took up this position in 1948, adopting the clerical soubriquet that he is known by. On October 18, 1950 he became an archbishop.

Among Cypriot Greeks, the Greek Orthodox Church is not only a source of spiritual guidance, but also a formidable political power. As an archbishop, Makarios at once became one of the most important players in the dramatic and bloody events of the 1950s on this very troubled island.

Makarios joined the clamor for union with Greece and very soon found himself at odds with the British authorities. He rejected Harding's proposals for a certain amount of autonomy and set his face firmly for *Enosis*. He was to disappoint fervent followers of *Enosis* later as president of the independent Republic of Cyprus, but at this time he became a thorn in the British side. Attempting to board a plane in Nicosia to parley with the Greek government on political union, the archbishop was arrested as an insurgent by Special Branch and dispatched to the Seychelles in what could not be seen as too hard an exile. Lord Mountbatten sent a warship to the Seychelles lest it be necessary to bring him back in style.

Anthony Eden fell from power when the military operations, launched from Cyprus, to secure the Suez Canal and to get rid of Gamal Abdel Nasser, failed. Harold Macmillan became prime minister with a very different approach to colonial affairs. His suggestion was that Turkey, Greece, and the UK should order the affairs of Cyprus in concert with the two main Cypriot communities. Greece declined, but Macmillan persisted and on October 1, 1958 negotiations aimed at this outcome commenced, with Greece feeling that she had no option but to attend. Whether or not the intention of the organizers of the negotiations, the British, was to walk backwards out of an expensive and blood-soaked situation and allow an independent Cyprus to emerge is not clear. But this is what happened.

Fellow NATO members Turkey and Greece have come close to war on several occasions since the organization was established in 1949. One of the flashpoints of mutual hostility has long been Cyprus and it has been in the interests of NATO as a whole to defuse tensions between these two members and to have a stable eastern Mediterranean dominated by NATO. The perennial issue of keeping Russia at bay was also a factor in defense policy.

A settlement of some sort was seen as necessary in relation to the island and the foreign secretaries of Greece and Turkey convened in Zurich to hammer out a plan for the founding of the Republic of Cyprus. By signing the resulting Zurich Agreement, composed of twenty-seven articles, on February 11, 1959, Turkish Prime Minister Adnan Menderes and Greek Prime Minister Karamanlis ensured that the new republic would come into being.

Conspicuous by his absence in Switzerland was Archbishop Makarios and this was one reason why EOKA was not placated by this ending of overall British rule. Violence continued. The reverend gentleman himself was positive about the outcome, publicly renounced *Enosis*, and returned to his homeland. He fully accepted the agreement.

Both Turkish and Greek leaders were invited to endorse these new arrangements by signing the London Agreement of February 19, 1959. A constitution was prepared, a power-sharing one based on what were (and often still are) seen as ethnic lines. Thus, Cyprus became a free sovereign nation at the stroke of midnight on August 16, 1960. Cypriots were to find that the arrangements had no element of panacea. Some may have fondly thought that the Greeks had put aside forever any hankering for *Enosis* and that Turkey had put aside the possibility of *Taksim*, or partition of the island. But this was not so.

Independence

The constitution of the Republic of Cyprus was a product of the Zurich and London Agreements and it became the basis of an uneasy settlement between the two main communities. Both Turkish and Greek speakers were recognized as coequal founders and partners of the new republic. The Chamber of Deputies was to consist of 30% Turkish and 70% Greek members. The Council of Ministers was to have three Turkish and seven Greek members. This proportion was also applied to municipalities. The balance in the police, the military police, and the military in general was set at 60% Greek and 40% Turkish. Contingents of 650 soldiers from Turkey and 950 soldiers from Greece were permitted to be stationed on the island for its defense. The UK, Turkey, and Greece became the guarantor nations, empowered with the right to intervene should the republic be in danger—either collectively or individually. A Turkish regiment and a Greek regiment duly took up stations on August 16, 1960.

Archbishop Makarios became the first president of the Republic of Cyprus while Dr. Fazıl Küçük, leader of the Turkish community of Cyprus, became vice president.

These dispositions were not to the satisfaction of all and no sooner had the ink dried on the constitution than movements were afoot aimed at its undoing. EOKA, as has been intimated, had not gone home to their mums and hung up their Sten guns just because British rule had ended. In addition to EOKA, EDMA (the National Democratic Fighters Front) and OPEK (the Organization for the Protection of Cypriot Greeks—a misnomer if ever there was one), resolved to overthrow the infant state. The last-named organization was led by one Nikos Sampson, a man who would make history and regret it. On the Turkish Cypriot side, TMT also declined to disband, and indeed consolidated its position with the covert support of Turkey.

With Makarios it is hard to see what his attitude to *Enosis* was, once in power. Had he really renounced it? Or had he only pretended to do so in order to get out of captivity? Certainly, he made pronouncements to the effect that *Enosis* was not dead in the water, that it was still a possible option. Flexibility may be the word to use here, but we could also use the word duplicity. Makarios toyed with both the wishes of many Cypriots to have a sovereign nation of their very own and the aspirations of many to unite with Greece. "The aim of this struggle is not founding the republic; these agreements have only laid down the foundations," he declared. Clearly, the settlement of 1960 was not to be seen as set in stone.

Bit by bit, Cypriot Turks started to realize that the brave new Cyprus was unlikely to go their way and that their new president did not necessarily have their best interests at heart. Constitutional rights were very clear on paper; in daily life—well, less so. EOKA continued its career of mayhem; Turkish municipalities found that they were not actually municipalities as stipulated by the constitution, but rather were inconvenient entities that many among their co-patriots wished would just go away.

It is not contended that right was on only one side and wickedness was a monopoly of the other. What is contended is that the boot, at this time, was firmly on the Greek foot. This led to something very frightening—the Akritas Plan.

The Akritas Plan

There have been many initiatives in history for the elimination of men, women, children, and babies in the "supposed" interests of the perpetrators. Elimination is the euphemism; the reality is mass murder.

So was it in Cyprus when a highly secret plan was put in place to undermine the republic. And to kill Cypriot Turks. The idea was to suggest a change in the constitution in the Cypriot Greeks' favor. Article Thirteen was to be amended—the article concerning free movement within the republic. When this would be (quite inevitably) opposed by the Turkish side, the pretext was (supposedly) there to take violent action and to pursue *Enosis*.

The plan was overseen by Polikarpos Yorgacis, Tassos Papadopoulos, and Glafkos Klerides. The idea was to respond to their own initiation of violence by staging a *coup d'état*. None of the plotters were under any illusions concerning the very strong opposition the Cypriot Turks would mount and this was to be crushed.

Makarios presented the guarantor countries with the blueprint for constitutional change and inevitably Turkey rejected it out of hand. Tediously and horrifically, EOKA swung into action once again. The ambitious game plan was to destroy the Turkish Cypriot community in one night. They should have done the math. The Akritas Plan was duly detonated on December 21, 1963. This day has gone down in history as Bloody Christmas.

The effect on Cypriot Turks was cataclysmic. An estimated 8,667 Cypriot Turks abandoned 103 villages to take refuge in six cantons. The number of internally displaced people subsequently rose to 25,000 or 30,000—due to the turmoil, exact figures were not gathered. The Turkish side lost 364, the Greek side 174. This was no longer intermittent terrorism, this was a massacre. Turkish jets flew over Nicosia on Christmas Day, which may have been the main factor in engineering a ceasefire. Yet this ceasefire was not to last.

Now a new era started for the Cypriot Turks: one of ordeal and pain and a struggle for survival. It lasted eleven years. As said above, the outside world had so often stepped in to dominate and exploit Cyprus, but this time it stayed away. Instead, Cypriot Turks had to call on their global contacts to seek opportunities for negotiation and remedy.

TMT and EOKA fought it out in an unequal conflict and the years passed in a situation that was not only unendurable, but also interminable.

On July 15, 1974 there was a genuine, not notional, *coup d'état* in the Republic of Cyprus. The name used by the perpetrators was "Operation Presidency." This name reflects the intention of killing the president. A usurper, the selfsame Nikos Sampson, was to take Makarios' place and declare the Republic of Cyprus likewise killed and a new "Hellenic Republic of Cyprus" born. With the far-right junta then in brutal charge of Greece behind him, he met with some success. Makarios wisely fled with the aid of the British and gained refuge in America.

Makarios had routinely commanded over 90% of the Greek Cypriot vote, so this coup created deep divisions within the Greek Cypriot community. Among the Cypriot Turks there was utter dismay.

The leader of the Turkish side, Rauf Denktaş, called upon Turkey to step in to fulfill her role as one of the guarantor powers (along with Greece and the UK). The constitution of 1960 was very clear regarding this right of intervention.

Giving a speech on July 19, 1974 at the UN Security Council, Makarios declared that:

> The coup caused much bloodshed and took a great toll of human lives. It was faced with the determined resistance of the legal security forces and the resistance of the Greek people of Cyprus. I can say with certainty that the resistance and the reaction of the Greek Cypriot people against the conspirators will not end until there is a restoration of their freedom and democratic rights. The Cypriot people will never bow to dictatorship even though for the moment the brutal force of the armored cars and tanks may have prevailed.

After the coup, the agents of the Greek regime in Cyprus appointed the aforementioned Nikos Sampson as president. He in turn appointed as ministers known elements and supporters of the terrorist organization "EOKA-B."

These are interesting actions from a former proponent of *Enosis*.

The "Cyprus Peace Operation" and the road to the Turkish Republic of Northern Cyprus

The coup against President Makarios and his administration had huge and lasting consequences. The Turkish government reacted swiftly. This was not just an attack on the Cyprus government and establishment, it was also an attack on the Turkish Cypriot community. Concerns were voiced that Turkish-speaking Cypriots would disappear. It was declared that a Greek invasion of the island had occurred. As with Makarios, the Turkish government had no sense that this was an internal power swap among Cypriots. Moves were afoot to intervene.

The Council of Ministers of the Republic of Turkey gathered on July 19, 1974 and gave full authority to Bülent Ecevit, then prime minister, to act against the Greek takeover. A negotiated settlement did not seem viable, especially after approaches to the UK, as a fellow guarantor, and to the Soviet Union proved fruitless.

On July 18, Turkish Prime Minister Ecevit sent Greece an ultimatum containing Turkey's demands. This ultimatum stipulated that Nikos Sampson renounce the presidency, that Greek military officers should be withdrawn from the island, and that independence be restored. The junta in Greece immediately rejected this. Upon this rejection, Turkey carried out the "Cyprus Peace Operation," as it is known in Turkey, on July 20, 1974, citing her right to intervene as guarantor. Landings by large numbers of troops were carried out on the northern coast of the island, with forces swiftly breaking out of the bridgeheads and fanning out inland. Having established herself formidably, Turkey agreed to the UN request for a cease-fire on the evening of July 22.

The fallout of these momentous events are still felt in Cyprus today. The bitter consequences of failure for the Greek government were felt immediately. As with the Argentinean junta after losing the Falklands War, their loss in Cyprus led the Greek people to tear down their junta. Nikos Sampson's momentary regime ended.

Following the ceasefire, a conference was convened in Geneva on July 25, 1974. The foreign ministers of Turkey, Greece, and the UK entered into talks aimed at ending the conflict. When the conference ended on July 30, Turkish demands for two autonomous administrations on the island had been accepted.

There was a problem. EOKA-B had not relinquished the positions they held, nor had they released the hostages they were holding. Turkey decided to end the ceasefire and to mount another offensive. Between August 14 and 16, Turkish forces pushed on further inland and established the line between the two sides that we see today.

Following the events of the sixty hot days of summer 1974, the Cypriot Turks declared the Turkish Federated State of Cyprus on February 13, 1975. While not happy with this declaration, the Cypriot Greeks felt compelled to attend meetings in Vienna held between April 28 and July 31. In the final meeting, the two sides came to an agreement on an envisaged voluntary population exchange. Cypriot Turks largely moved north and Cypriot Greeks largely moved south—if they had not done so already. This exchange took place in September 1975. And thus, Cyprus divided effectively into two autonomous states with two distinct communities.

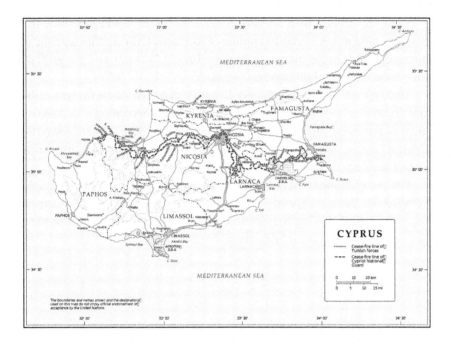

Upon the death of Archbishop Makarios on August 3, 1977, Spyros Kyprianou, leader of the Democratic Party, was elected president of Cyprus by the Cypriot Greeks. The Turkish Federated State of Cyprus and Turkey did not acknowledge his presidency, stating that Kyprianou represented the Cypriot Greeks only and, consequently, held sway on that part of the island only.

Inter-communal negotiations languidly continued. The Cypriot Greeks and Greece succeeded in carrying their issues to international arenas. Thus, they managed to elicit a decision, dated May 13, 1983 at the United Nations, calling for the dissolution of the Turkish Federated State of Cyprus (TFSC). Turkey, Pakistan, Bangladesh, Malaysia, and Somalia voted against this decision in the UN Security Council. In this decision, numbered 37/253, the sovereignty, independence, territorial integrity, unity, and non-alignment of the Republic of Cyprus were supported. All acts aimed at violating these rights were to be condemned. The president proposed demilitarization of the island, with all foreign troops being asked to depart. However, this did not happen; nor did a breakthrough in negotiations concerning final status Therefore, on November 15, 1983, the parliament of the Turkish Federated State of Cyprus proclaimed the Turkish Republic of Northern Cyprus (TRNC). This remains the existing state of affairs.

With the election held on June 9, 1985, Rauf Raif Denktaş became the first president of the Turkish Republic of Northern Cyprus. This republic is not recognized. The initial recognition by Turkey, Pakistan, and Bangladesh was renounced after international pressure.

The Cypriot Turks on the island demonstrated their desire for reconciliation by voting "yes" in a referendum held in 2004 concerning a final settlement brokered by the UN under General Secretary Kofi Annan. Alas, the Cypriot Greeks, due to concerns of their own, voted the whole thing down and so nothing changed.

Peace negotiations have been in train since 1968. The negotiations between the Turkish Cypriot people's leader, Mustafa Akıncı, who assumed the presidency following the election of 2015, and the Greek Cypriot people's leader, Nicos Anastasiades, are still ongoing.

CHAPTER ONE

Rengin—a bus ride

Vamık Volkan, aged 1 and aged 4, Nicosia, Cyprus.

In his article "Mourning and melancholia," Sigmund Freud (1917e) remarks that we cannot willingly give up on our emotional bonds with the deceased. He explains the fact that we are bereft does not mean we have given up our interest in the departed and he states that we continue a kind of relationship through emotion.

As for Vamık Volkan, he uses the expression "psychic double" to clarify this. Rather like a child with an imaginary friend, someone who has lost a loved one will always keep images in their mind. The patterns differ with age. A child of one or two who loses a mother will not be able to store images or maintain a psychic double in the same way as an older child who has had more time to form and maintain images.

Psychoanalysts call this critical skill to form and store the other's psychic double or representation in the mind the "object constancy." The object constancy enables a child to endure the times he (let us allow the single gender to apply to both) is alone by giving him a chance to store a set of characters in his mind, which is actually storing the images in the mind. As the child develops, his ability to store and maintain the psychic doubles of the departed grows stronger, and he manages to stay alone for longer periods of time. This is an important process and we

Vamık Volkan (middle) with sisters Tomris (left) and Sevim (right), taken 1938.

can speculate that adults who find it difficult to be on their own did not undergo this process adequately.

In Dr. Volkan's opinion, the concept of the psychic double has to be properly perceived if one wants to understand mourning. We are affected by our ongoing relationships in the real world. We are affected by each and every person we meet and we review the psychic double accordingly. However, when a person close to us dies, our real-world life is diminished. Even so, the psychic double goes on. We can even say that the bond intensifies due to the physical separation. Yet this is not permanent and the act of mourning tends to lessen the pain of loss and to lessen dependence on the psychic double (Volkan, 1981; Volkan & Zintl, 1999).

One of the memories that Vamık Volkan holds from his childhood concerns Rengin. Rengin was a cat fed and cared for by Vamık's family. Vamık's father was a teacher in Malia, now a village in southern Cyprus. The family set out for Nicosia by bus, the most usual form of transport at that time. Rengin was in Vamık's arms on the bus, but then leapt out and disappeared into the hazy morning. A search ensued and they could find no trace of Rengin. Here we see the first experience of loss that Vamık Volkan had, just before school age. It has stayed with him.

Our ways of mourning are as particular to us as our fingerprints. Although families may share characteristics and behavioral patterns in this respect, sorrow is deeply personal. We can also say that we are all to an extent composites of those we have lost.

Vamık Volkan experienced a painful loss six months after taking up residence in the USA in early 1957 that has still not left him. His father sent him a newspaper clipping with the news. It concerned his roommate from his medical school days in Ankara, who had returned to Cyprus to tend to his ailing mother. His name was Erol Mulla and he was like a brother to Vamık Volkan. Erol was shot and killed by an EOKA terrorist in a chemist shop in Güzelyurt (Morphou by its former name) when he went there to buy medication for his mother. The EOKA gunman, who was never identified, targeted Erol for the sole purpose of terrorizing the ethnic group to which Erol Mulla and Vamık Volkan belonged.

Erol was to become, posthumously, one of the main influences on Vamık Volkan's formulation of psychoanalytical and psychopolitical concepts.

CHAPTER TWO

Father's memoirs

Ahmet Cemal (1899–1970), Vamık Volkan's father. Picture taken in 1948.

Fatma Ahmet Cemal (1903–1979), Vamık Volkan's mother. Picture taken in 1948.

Whenhen writing a biography of a psychoanalyst, it is perhaps more of a necessity than usual to outline his childhood, his family, and, in particular, his parents. With that in mind, here is a chapter on Vamık Volkan's father, Ahmet Cemal. As, after all, the narrative of the father lives on in the life of the son.

Ahmet Cemal, started to write about his professional life of forty years' standing in 1959 while he was headteacher at Köşklüçiftlik Primary School in Nicosia. Two years previously, Vamık had graduated from Ankara University Medical School and had gone to the USA to pursue a further education in psychiatry and psychoanalysis. He had little hope of returning to Cyprus in the near future due to the deteriorating political situation and yet, after some years, he did come back.

In 1968 the enclaved Cypriot Turks found that they could exit the various areas they were hemmed into if they met certain criteria. Taking advantage of this opportunity, Vamık came to Cyprus with his wife. Family members were at Nicosia Airport to welcome them and to take them to the Turkish side of the city by car. Vamık was struck by the tense silence in the car. Afterwards, he realised that this was due to the fact that his folks were unused to being in Greek-controlled places and that they were so frightened they actually whispered, in spite of being in the confines of the vehicle. After crossing to the Turkish district of the city, normal conversation was resumed.

A lot had changed by the time of this family reunion. Vamık had received a great deal of education in psychoanalysis and he had also undergone psychoanalysis himself as part of this process. As a result, it had become clear to him how pivotal a role his father had held in the development of his character. He found that his identity was bound up with his childhood fantasies about his father and he very much wanted to talk to him about them. However, his father lost his memory that year; there was no medical diagnosis for this. When his father died two years later, Vamık was away from the island.

Having spent all his life on the island, Ahmet Cemal switched citizenship several times, as did many in that time. First, he was an Ottoman, then British, then a citizen of the Republic of Cyprus, and, finally, by the time of his death, he was a citizen of the Turkish Federated State of Cyprus. And today, he rests in Nicosia Cemetery in the Turkish Republic of Northern Cyprus.

Vamık knew that his father had written his memoirs and when he began to come to Cyprus more frequently, his sisters gave him the manuscript. This manuscript came to have an importance comparable with that of a holy scripture for him. He started making his own notes on the subject of his father's life and he contacted other Cypriot Turks on the importance of his father's work.

One aspect of the work in question concerned the rise in religious education in Northern Cyprus. With all the changes on the island the question "Who are we now?" arose. The memoirs not only outline his father's life and career, but also constitute a disquisition on the role of religion among the Cypriots at the start of the twentieth century. He writes of the conflict between Turkish teachers who adopted secularism and imams (small-time religious leaders). Vamık tells of the necessity of sharing these memoirs:

> Along with pressure to be a "Cypriot" an idea also develops that the Turks and the Greeks on Cyprus have lived together as brothers and sisters for centuries. Even though my father does not dwell much upon Turkish–Greek relations, he gives an example of the separation between the Turkish Cypriots and the Greek Cypriots and tells about the effects of this separation on those who follow the new Turkish identity created by Mustafa Kemal Atatürk and his associates.

* * *

Tziaos is a Turkish village with a population of around 1,000 settled to the north of the sixteenth mile of the asphalt road to Nicosia from Rizokarpaso.

Thus begins Ahmet Cemal's memoirs, penned from 1959 onwards. This is where he was born. The village has quite a history and there have been many findings from Venetian times, for this was a Venetian village. When the Venetians departed Cyprus, the village was abandoned. It was resettled by Turkish people from northern Anatolia and these are the ancestors of the present villagers. At the time of Ahmet Cemal's writing the village had a police station, a cinema, a market, a flour plant, a Cooperative office, a Cooperative grocery, barns, a telephone, a primary school with three teachers, many fountains, a few gardens, prickly pears, and other fruit trees. He further states that the people of Tziaos were quite hospitable and they enjoyed feeding and hosting guests in their homes. Most were either farmers or shepherds. Ahmet Cemal's father was a farmer.

Ahmet Cemal documents his own birth:

> Exactly 60 years ago, a boy approached my father as he was leaving the mosque in Tziaos village in the Province of Famagusta on the twenty-eighth day of September 1899 at 2pm and said "Good news. Your lady has had a boy." I became the first son but the fourth child of the family. My father rewarded the boy who gave him the good news—because I was a boy.

Ahmet Cemal discusses various educational issues of the period. Around the beginning of the twentieth century there were turbaned teachers teaching in the Turkish Cypriot villages. These men (they were all men) used the old Turkish and Islamic catechisms, gave importance to the study of the Quran, as well as grammar and algebra. The children gathered in their classrooms at lesson times and sat on straw mats on the floor. Discipline was harsh. The teachers had canes by their desks and should a pupil create a disturbance, or be deemed lazy, punishment was swift. Children were caned on their hands, their shoulders, and their heads. When a teacher really lost his temper, he might slap a pupil in the face. Also, each school had a ball of black stone which weighed about five kilograms and students would be punished by being made to stand on one foot for an hour holding the ball on the left shoulder with the left hand and holding the right foot with the right hand. If the stone fell, the punishment would be extended for another hour. There were also collective punishments. If one pupil was deemed to have sinned in some way, often enough all were lined up for corporal punishment. There was also a rather bizarre form of treatment of supposed malefactors. Teachers had a metal object on the heels of their shoes, something like a horseshoe, the purpose of which was to inflict pain. At a command, pupils would have to place their hands on the desks. The teacher would then mount the desks and walk on the children's hands. Sometimes a twist of the heel would make the pain a little more exquisite. A horseshoe shape was imprinted on the hapless hands as if to set a seal to this dreadful purpose. In the event of an act of impertinence, yet harsher punishments were dealt out.

Ahmet Cemal states in his memoirs that despite all the above, he took a liking to the school and that he could still recall things he memorized, albeit without knowing the meaning.

He left primary school at the end of 1911 and went on to high school and the madrasa.

Torment for the children was not to remain a thing of the past as they moved up. The methods of punishment were just different. Pupils were caned either on their thighs or the soles of their feet. This latter practice is called *falaka* in this part of the world. When a child was to undergo *falaka*, all the pupils in the school would gather in the hall to witness punishment. His shoes would be removed and the schoolmaster would hit the soles of his feet with a thick cane as much as he felt inclined.

Detention was a less physically painful but arduous sanction. Some were not allowed home for their lunch break, some were kept in after school hours and forced to write lines on the blackboard 600 times. Presumably the need to erase lines to make space for more added to the miserable sense of the futility of this rigmarole.

In the case of misdeeds deemed to be more heinous, a child might be suspended for a week or two, or might even be expelled. Whilst this may sound more of a boon than a punishment, alternatives in education were scarce. Thus, the local children received their schooling in an atmosphere of fear.

After leaving his local high school in 1916, Ahmet Cemal went to Nicosia High School. Nicosia was the capital, but was a town of only 13,000 souls at this time. Things were not easy. The First World War was raging and while unscathed by attack, conditions were not good. Cyprus has never been immune to the travails of the outside world.

Vamık Volkan:

> What really sparks my attention is that my father hardly mentions the Cypriot Greeks and the Greek Cypriot students while he tells about his life in secondary and high school. From what he writes, I developed the idea that the Turkish primary school and high school students living in Nicosia had nothing to do with the Cypriot Greeks. The Turkish Cypriot students and the Greek Cypriot students completed their education without getting to know each other.

Ahmet Cemal decided to become a teacher after high school. Having made the necessary applications, he was appointed to a school in Kampyli, a village with a population of 240, boasting no fewer than twenty-two Turkish and three Maronite (Syriac Christian) pupils. He expressed joy:

> Let me describe my enthusiasm for teaching even at my tender age. I would gather the kids in my own house, taking attendance and I would give lessons there. I was very highly motivated.

Although Ahmet Cemal loved teaching, it proved a struggle early on. His predecessor had been a turbaned individual who preached and prayed and prepared amulets for the villagers. This was a practice which was common in other villages too and young teachers with modern ideas saw this as rather vexatious.

Ahmet Cemal's second posting was to the village of Pınarlı. He notes that the number of Greek Cypriot families was forty-one when he started teaching there and then the number increased to eighty. He attributes this situation to the Cypriot government taking educational management into its own hands. On the one hand, this exacerbated the discrimination between the Greek and the Turkish populations, while on the other it widened the rift between imams and young, officially appointed teachers.

Ahmet Cemal moved to Limassol as a progression of his teaching career and was then assigned, in turn, to Nicosia High School and the village school in Epicho. At this time, the mid 1920s, the Republic of Turkey passed legislation banning the fez, a hat which Atatürk deemed symbolic of hidebound ways and men were encouraged to wear Western-style hats and Western dress in general. Ahmet Cemal duly adopted the Western hat habit.

Having never discovered the reason why he was suddenly appointed to Epicho from Nicosia, Ahmet Cemal speculates in his memoirs that this had something to do with the Turkish reforms concerning clothing. The religious conservatives and the secularists within the Turkish community in Cyprus were diverging rapidly. It is possible that Ahmet Cemal was redeployed as a progressive influence in a more conservative place.

Vamık Volkan:

> When I read my father's memoirs and understood the struggles he faced as a teacher, I realized once again the importance of the role religious beliefs had in the fall of the Ottoman Empire and how important the reforms Atatürk initiated were for the future of the

Turkish people. One of the reforms concerned clothing. Some of the steps taken by Atatürk might seem insignificant to some, but those steps had revolutionary implications at that period. What attracts my attention is the immediate adoption of the revolutionary ways in train in Turkey by the youth living under British rule in Cyprus—by my father, among many.

Determined to change the dress style of the Turkish people, Atatürk left Ankara with his friend Nuri Conker and others in the morning of 25th August 1925 and headed for Kastamonu, recognized as among the most conservative cities in Turkey at that time. The local people welcomed their visitors in large numbers and were presumably surprised when Atatürk pointed to his panama hat and said, "This is called a hat." My father wrote in his memoirs that he was one of the first hat-wearers among the Cypriot Turks. My father explains that the reason why he so quickly accepted the hat reform concerned an event he experienced in his childhood which highlighted the separation between the Cypriot Turks and the Cypriot Greeks.

Ahmet Cemal:

I had adopted the type of hat that was accepted by all nations at a young age. Why? One day, when I was a child, I took my father to the train station on a mule, as he was to journey to Famagusta, after which I rode home. I had a fez on my head. To get back to my village, I had to go through Maratha, which is a Greek village. When I got to Maratha, I felt a sudden frisson of fear: what if the Greek boys beat me up? Sometimes your fears come true. Mine certainly did. When the Greek boys saw me with the fez on, they started to chase me, throwing stones. They threw stones at me until I had left the village, but they never managed to score a hit. That's because I could ride well. Nonetheless, I was very frightened. A thought occurred to me when I had got out of danger—"Why can't all nations wear the same things so that no one's national garb can make them stand out?" I assumed that had I been wearing a Western-style hat rather than a fez, I would not have had this frightening experience. With this in mind, I wore a Western-style hat as soon as the hat reform was in place.

Vamık Volkan has in his possession the first sixty-three pages of his father's memoirs. The rest are lost. The extant manuscript ends with the sentence, "How did the hat issue get resolved?"

The memoirs were being kept in the house of Vamık's sister Tomris Güney when the troubles erupted in Cyprus in December 1963 (Bloody Christmas), and as with so many Turkish houses, Tomris' house was attacked and sacked. This appears to be why the remaining pages of the manuscript did not survive.

The hat issue was resolved most positively, albeit slowly. Vamık recalls that his father emulated Atatürk by going into the village coffee house and, pointing to his hat, repeated Atatürk's words, "Gentlemen, this is called a hat." As Tomris remembers it, nearly all the men in the village had started to wear hats by the time her father left Epicho.

Although Vamık's father was among the first Turkish hat-wearers, his mother only stopped wearing the chador as late as the 1940s. This was due to a facet of human nature rather than to religious beliefs. Ahmet Cemal was jealous about his wife and wanted to hide her from other men.

CHAPTER THREE

Vignettes of life

Vamık Volkan drew his first breath in the year 1932. He was the last child of the family. He lived in an average home for the time and he shared it with his sisters Sevim and Tomris, who were respectively five and six years older than him.

His sister Tomris Güney was among the first to witness her brother's advent. When I interviewed her on July 1, 2014, I asked her to share this with me. She replied:

> Vamık was born in Nicosia. When my mum and my grandmother and the midwife went into a room of the two-roomed house where we lived back in those days on Abdi Çavuş Street for the delivery, we children were told to wait in the opposite room. So we waited. We spent that time playing games, with little concentration. Every once in a while, my grandmother came in and made sure we were sitting quietly and she told us stories. My mother's labor-induced cries rose from the other room. Although my grandmother occasionally went in and out, we were kept waiting. Then my grandmother came back and told us, "We have a boy." I was very happy. I rushed in to see. Vamık was there and he turned out to be blond boy with blue eyes. He was a beautiful boy.

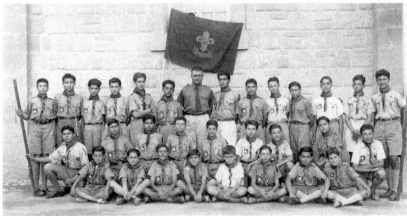

Vamık Volkan at high-school age in the boy scouts.

Vamık grew up in a family in which his mother was a teacher and a principal, his father was a teacher and a principal, and his two sisters were teachers. His childhood was spent in constant relocation due to his father's appointments to different places on the island. So, he grew up in Tziaos, Epicho, Knodara, Malia, and Nicosia. Mostly experiencing village life, Vamık had a fun-filled, fulfilling childhood and his memories are bright—riding on the neighbor's ram, playing hide and seek, and other such innocent pleasures.

Vamık tells of an incident in his very early years which is etched on his memory.

> One morning when I was two, I got kidnapped in front of our home in Nicosia by a Greek woman. The aim was not ransom. Nor did this poor woman have any intention of hurting me; she actually wanted to raise me as her own son. She was not the smartest person around and she had the soubriquet "Tasiya the mad." Her endeavor was short-lived and I was found in the afternoon at the power station in Nicosia where she had hidden me. I have no memory of this part of the event, but I can remember the anxiety-ridden expression my mother and grandmother had on their faces while they were telling and reliving the story. I was entranced by this story. This incident became a myth in my mind. When I grew a little older, I speculated that I could well have been electrocuted, but I also felt a frisson of pleasure to think that I was desired by a Greek person as a Turkish child.

War

As Vamık says, during his early years there was little violence between Cypriot Greeks and Turks, but once again an outside threat reared its head and the Nazis most certainly practiced violence. When Crete, another Mediterranean island of similar size to Cyprus, was invaded by Germany in 1941 with the British and Commonwealth forces in full flight, the fear was that Cyprus would be next. Vamık was too young to fully comprehend the danger, but he recalls the high drama of the times. A shelter was dug in the backyard and when the sirens screamed the family would take cover there. Food was rationed and they were forced to eat dark, tasteless bread. The family had to learn how to put on a gas mask, an ominous task. They noticed turbaned Indian Sikh soldiers of the British Army walking around their neighborhood. While Vamık was playing with other kids in the school yard, he witnessed a British Spitfire downing an Italian warplane. It could be said the Cypriot Turks and the Cypriot Greeks had mutual "masters" during his childhood period and, by extension, mutual enemies. These masters were the British and their foreign enemies were the Germans and the Italians among others.

In this time of hostility, love could nevertheless bloom with its usual unexpectedness.

Vamık Volkan:

> A mud brick wall separated my house and that of Elena's, daughter of a Greek Cypriot family, and when I grew taller I started to see Elena in the yard over the wall. I don't know when we met for the first time, but we must have come across each other in front of our homes. I used to point at a car or a bike in the street and tell her the Turkish words for them and she tried to teach me their Greek names in return. After a while we both reached adolescence and we accepted that our friendship was considered taboo by our cultures—cultures that forbade marriages between two groups almost as adamantly as they forbade incest. Without realizing it, I experienced at first hand how large-group identities divide people.
>
> There was only one English school in Nicosia to which both Cypriot Turks and Greeks went at this time. The respective communities were generally educated in their own idiom—separately. I received my high school education in Turkish and although there were Greeks all around the island and I came across them every day without any negative prejudgment, I never learned how to speak Greek. We were different, but we were all human beings.

Higher education and causal relationships

> I was born over eighty years ago. The Cyprus I grew up in was so much different then. We were not rich. We lived in a rented house. I didn't leave this island for eighteen years; going to Ankara after I finished high school seemed like a very big deal. That was the first time I left Cyprus.
>
> I would get back to Cyprus for summer holidays. I graduated in June 1956 and I was able to return to Cyprus. I had the option of opening a clinic and practicing medicine in this way. But I never thought of doing anything like that over the course of my education. Everyone in my family was a teacher. My sisters, my father, my mother were all teachers while my uncle was a doctor in medical school. That was always in my mind. I had most certainly not studied medicine in order to open a clinic.

Why did I choose psychiatry? I repeatedly asked myself this question for twenty-five years or so. Why did I study medicine and what was my underlying motivation to go to the USA?

When I was in medical school, we had a teacher called Rasim Adasal. Everyone knew Rasim Adasal. The radio was the main modern medium at that time and newspapers were read over the radio. Professor Adasal was popular in the media and he wrote various articles. He was from Crete and he spoke Turkish with an accent which was different from any prevailing in Turkey. Maybe it was not like the Cypriot dialect, but he spoke with an island accent. I really identified with him. This man went around saying "I am the Turkish Freud."

He was both a professor and head of psychiatry. Another important thing about him for me was that he was a friend of my uncle's, whom I revered. And my uncle was by then the famous eye doctor Cahit Örgen. Because he was a friend of my uncle's and my uncle was important to me and because of his position in the school, I started to see Professor Rasim as a charismatic man, one to know. As I say, I was only able to make this analysis twenty or twenty-five years later. This professor, who never got married, was an author of psychiatry textbooks. Most titles were on psychoanalytic subjects.

When I look back now, I see that Professor Rasim Adasal was not someone who deeply examined and studied psychoanalysis. But he was the one who brought psychoanalysis to Ankara University Medical School. I did not know very much about the subject, but it seems that he did not either. His content was superficial. Yet, I was inspired by him. Possibly paradoxically, if Professor Adasal had properly understood the concepts of psychoanalysis, I might not have been inspired in this field. I wouldn't have felt the need to study more deeply. Because of the books he wrote so superficially, I couldn't learn psychoanalysis from him. For this reason I turned my own hand to it. I still have some of his books in my house.

Replacement child

Vamık's name has an unusual provenance.

They gave me the name Ömer Vamık when I was born. Later, when I had to go to Turkey, I needed a surname. In those years, there was no law or obligation enforcing the use of surnames in Cyprus. Part of Turkey's modernization program was the adoption of surnames. While I was considering surnames with my sisters, one of them looked at the Kyrenia Mountains and said, "You, too, will erupt like a volcano [Volkan in Turkish]." That's how I got the surname Volkan; there was no one named Volkan in the family.

I was not initially aware of the underlying reason for my career as a psychiatrist and then as a psychoanalyst, or even for my studies into large-group psychology. Yet, as my professional capabilities grew, I examined myself in this respect.

My mother's grandfather, Ömer Vamık, was the last Ottoman jurist of Nicosia. Ömer Vamık was a powerful and influential man. But when the British came, things changed for my mother's grandfather as well as for many other Ottoman personnel on the island. They sent Ömer Vamık to a place near Lefke, in the west of the island. Ömer Vamık had twelve stores in the Ömerge neighborhood, which is now on the Greek side. The family was rich. The British came to the island and impoverished these people. So we were not rich when I was born.

My mother was the eldest child. The second eldest was my uncle Ömer Vamık, then my uncle Cemil and my uncle Cahit. Uncle Ömer Vamık was found dead in the Sea of Marmara after he had gone to Istanbul to study engineering. They only found his body fifty-three days after his death. He was identified thanks to my uncle Cemil's watch which he had on his wrist. It is still not certain under what circumstances my uncle died.

One of the things I remembered and was affected by for all my childhood is that my grandmother, the mother of my uncle Ömer Vamık, used to go into a darkened room into which no one else would go and open a particular bundle and start to lament. It was a bundle of things that had belonged to my uncle.

There is something in psychoanalysis called the "replacement child." Someone dies and then another child who is born later is perceived, most often unconsciously, as the dead person and upon the newborn child is imposed a duty to keep the dead "alive"—the replacement child.

I went through psychoanalysis for years and then I thought over these things much later on my own. Considering all that, I can say that I'm an unadulterated replacement child. I carry the name Ömer Vamık that belonged to both my great great grandfather and to my uncle. I was also assigned from my mother's side a duty to bring back the old prestige of being an Ottoman Cypriot Turk.

Vamık Volkan associates a significant part of his life with this duty for which he was destined from birth. He has felt it his task to uphold the names of his family's great great grandfather and of his prematurely deceased uncle.

CHAPTER FOUR

Coming to the USA and later on

Cherry Hospital highway historical marker, Goldsboro, NC.

When Vamık Volkan left Turkey in early 1957 for the USA, armed with his medical degree from Ankara University, the motivation to so do was twofold. The first was soul-searching about his father sending him an allowance; this gave him the sense that he was a burden on his family. The second factor was a strong suspicion that he would be unable to rise as an academic in Turkey as one with British nationality. Indeed, when he became a university assistant upon graduation in Ankara, he was unable to obtain a work permit due to his UK nationality, nor, crucially, could he draw a salary. He applied to the Lutheran Deaconess Hospital in Chicago and was accepted and set off with a small item of luggage, fifteen dollars, and his violin. This transition in his life left one thing by the wayside which he has regretted ever since—actually playing the violin.

As with so many other families at the time, Vamık's parents sent him to violin lessons with the renowned teacher Vahan Bedelyan, and bought him his first violin. Vahan Bedelyan was a violin virtuoso and tutor of Armenian origin (Volkan, 2019). In an interview years later, Vamık said that the most conspicuous regret of his life was "giving up playing the violin."

Dr. Volkan's departure for the USA was a part of the phenomenon known as the "brain drain." Out of eighty graduates of his medical school, half went to America. The USA had a lack of medical doctors at this time and they attracted many from around the world. The Cypriot Greeks, who were then struggling against British rule in order to unite Cyprus with Greece, began to oppress the Cypriot Turks as well as attacking the UK's forces and civilians. Vamık's departure for America coincided with this period.

Landing in New York, a burly man carried his suitcase for him and then demanded a tip. Vamık was short of funds and declined to hand over the money. He recalls being showered with curses and having to take it all quietly. Such was his first experience of the United States. His second was better. After this ugly scene he entered a room in which he saw a television for the first time in his life.

On arriving in Chicago, Dr. Volkan inquired as to how much a cab ride to his destination—the Lutheran Deaconess Hospital—would cost. Happy to hear that it would only take five of his dwindling supply of dollars, he accepted and duly arrived at his new workplace, introduced himself, and was shown to his room. This was plagued by noise, being immediately above the accident and emergency section of the hospital. The hospital catered for around 600 patients. Dr. Volkan found himself on night duty the very next day, but got through it with the help of the nurses. And as the weeks went by, he found his feet.

Two weeks later a troubling thing happened in the hospital. A surgeon in charge of administration gathered the newcomers to explain to his assistant doctors from other parts of the world what a telephone was. This struck Dr. Volkan as a kind of humiliation ceremony.

As mentioned in Chapter One, news of the untimely death of his friend Erol arrived by letter from Vamık's father. This would be a sad spur for him to reintroduce and enlarge on Freud's work on mourning. Yet it was not easy to pursue the mourning process himself. As he puts it:

> I had a Hungarian doctor friend with whom I shared a room. He was very troubled in relation to his family. His wife and children took refuge in the USA following the Hungarian Uprising and its crushing by the Soviets. But one of the children, his firstborn, had been left behind. She only managed to come to the USA a year later. Together, we went through the most chaotic time of his life. In addition to this, the myriad problems in the hospital on the one hand and the fact that I couldn't mourn for Erol on the other, rather blighted my life.

It was in conversations such as these where the years would fall away and I could see another time in his eyes:

> The world is changing fast. The plans we made in our youth are obsolete. In those days there were no computers, no electronic media, no cornucopia of technological devices that we see today. Social frameworks and political outlooks have changed both individually and globally along with our personal perspectives. Over time, we have changed, too.

And the course of Dr. Volkan's career was no exception. He also saw a gaping chasm open between his childhood dreams and his adult career. His career over his working life has been in three main fields. These are psychiatry/psychoanalysis, hospital management, and large-group psychology. He spent a fairly long time in Turkey to prepare himself for psychoanalysis, which was the first field he specialized in. By going to the USA as a newly graduated doctor he resumed his education, something which was always in his mind. After interning at the Lutheran Deaconess Hospital in Chicago, he started his psychiatry education in the Memorial Hospital of North Carolina University in Chapel Hill. Then he worked for a few years in Cherry Hospital, a state psychiatric hospital in Goldsboro, North Carolina, that catered exclusively to African Americans. He then worked at the Dorothea Dix Hospital in Raleigh, which was only for white Americans. After staying in North Carolina for five years, he started to work in psychiatry at the University of Virginia School of Medicine in Charlottesville in 1964.

After settling in Charlottesville, he completed his psychoanalysis education at the Washington Psychoanalytic Institute in Washington D.C.

> I remember traveling between Charlottesville and Washington for many hours for my psychoanalysis education in the Washington Psychoanalytic Institute and lying on my psychoanalyst's couch for my own analysis four times a week. At this time Highway 29 (connecting Charlottesville to Washington) was still composed of two lanes instead of four.

After nearly two decades of education and professional development, in 1974 Dr. Volkan became a member of the American Psychiatric Association. Feeling comfortable and satisfied in practicing psychoanalysis as a faculty member of the Department of Psychiatry at the University of Virginia, he also had administrative duties such as being the director of the psychiatric inpatient service and the acting chairman of his department. After some years he was appointed medical director of the Blue Ridge Hospital, a general hospital of the University of Virginia with 600 beds, while still continuing his psychoanalytic practice and teaching. His academic career at the University of Virginia lasted from 1963 to 2002; and for eighteen years he remained medical director of the Blue Ridge Hospital. His first career was his becoming a physician and psychoanalyst; his second career was to function as an administrator.

In contrast with the long years very consciously spent becoming a psychoanalyst and a manager of a medical practice, Dr. Volkan was entirely unprepared for the title of "political psychologist." He had not pursued this and it took some time of being called this by various people in the academic and political milieu before he too acknowledged the title. This new departure was more or less accidental. Those who want a career in politics and international affairs do not generally go through a psychiatric or psychoanalytic education. Similarly, psychiatric or psychoanalytic educations do not include subjects associated with politics and international affairs. That said, some psychoanalysts since Sigmund Freud have shown an interest in the relationships between political leaders and their followers and in subjects such as human behavior in religion and in large groups and when at war. The American Psychiatric Association founded its Psychiatry and Foreign Affairs Committee in the 1970s. This was a team composed of psychiatrists who were interested in the USA's domestic and foreign policies, or who got involved in these things for personal reasons, but who did not have a special theory or particular methods for studying the psychological background of these matters. Dr. Volkan was invited to join this committee.

When I was asked to join this committee in 1978, I was excited and flattered. A couple of months later, Demetrios Julius, a Greek-born American psychiatrist, became a member of the committee.

After what was anyway a long and difficult history, Turkish–Greek relations became rather more tense towards the end of 1978. The Ottoman Turks, my ancestors, had conquered Cyprus from the Venetian Empire between the years 1570 and 1571. Throughout the Venetian period, the Greek Orthodox Church was oppressed as the Venetians attempted to impose Roman Catholicism upon Cyprus. The Ottomans accepted the Greek Orthodox Church as the only non-Muslim religious organization on the island and restored it to its former stature. Although the island belonged to the Ottomans, on the agreement of the Sultan in 1878, the Ottomans handed over its administration to Great Britain. In return, the British helped the Ottomans defend themselves against the Russians. Even though it was considered Ottoman territory in name during this period, Cyprus was finally annexed by the British at the start of World War I in 1914. The Turkish Republic, which was founded in the wake of the collapse of the Ottoman Empire, recognized British rule in Cyprus.

As the brief history above shows, the Cypriot Turks and the Cypriot Greeks of my childhood had lived for almost 400 years under Ottoman or British rule subject to strict centralized control. Throughout this era, Cypriot Turks and Cypriot Greeks lived by the cultural and social rules created by a single central authority.

The British administration on the island ended in 1960 and the Republic of Cyprus was founded as a controversial entity that attempted to create a political partnership between the Cypriot Turks and the Cypriot Greeks. Three years later, the Cypriot Turks were forced by the Cypriot Greeks to live in a few enclaves covering only three percent of the island under inhumane conditions for eleven years. The Turkish armed forces arrived on the island in 1974 and the island was de facto divided into the northern Turkish part and the southern Greek part.

At the time when Demetrios and I were invited onto the committee, peace had not been established between the Cypriot Turks and the Cypriot Greeks, or more widely, between Turkey and Greece.

I gradually started to feel that even though the senior members of the committee were mostly kind towards the new Greek-American and Turkish-American members, we both, Demetrios as a Greek-American born in Greece and me, as a Turkish-American, were selected as "guinea pigs" to be observed by the other committee members.

I realized that our invitation to join the committee was not because of our capabilities in political psychology or in international affairs but because of our ethnic identities. As a matter of fact, I took kindly to being a guinea pig. I found myself thinking about why this new development in my professional life excited me so much. I started a kind of self-analysis.

Vamık links his childhood experiences with his relationship with the APA's committee.

I realized I'd never had a Greek friend in all my adult life. After the division of the island into the Turkish and Greek sides in 1974, I knew the Cyprus of my childhood was gone forever, and of course, points of contact between the two sides were few. When I was offered membership of the APA's committee, I believed the idea of working with a Greek-American psychiatrist would awaken in me a nostalgia for the lost Cyprus of my childhood where the Turkish and the Greek people lived side by side.

CHAPTER FIVE

Friendship with Denktaş

Rauf Denktaş and Vamık Volkan in 1988 at Kyrenia, North Cyprus.

Vamık Volkan was a friend of Rauf Denktaş and his family for many years.

Rauf Raif Denktaş was born on January 27, 1924 in Paphos, Cyprus. He was destined to assume the leadership of the Turkish community of Cyprus between February 28, 1973 and April 24, 2005. These were the periods of the Autonomy, the Federation, and the Republic.

Rauf Denktaş was the son of a judge. He was raised by his grandmothers after he lost his mother when he was one and a half years old. He was sent to Istanbul for his education in 1930. He attended boarding school from primary level to high school. He returned to Cyprus thereafter and graduated from The English School, Nicosia and started to write articles for newspapers. He then left for England to study law at Lincoln's Inn, returning to the island in 1947 to become a lawyer, after which he became a public prosecutor. By 1956 he was chief public prosecutor.

He took a firm stance on the side of the Cypriot Turks in the Greek-on-Turkish conflict that had started by this time. Upon decolonization he took office in the newly independent administration of the Republic of Cyprus. Then, when the Republic fell, he carried on the struggle for Turkish rights on the island and eventually became the leader of this struggle. When the island was divided by the events of 1974, Rauf Denktaş became the leader of the Turkish Cypriot administration in the northern third of the island and then became the founding president of the Turkish Republic of Northern Cyprus in 1983, albeit without global recognition. He died on January 13, 2012 in Nicosia.

The friendship between the two men coincided with the Denktaş administration of this period. Over the course of their friendship they shared the grief of losing a child and they conferred on the political intricacies arising from the newly established republic, problematic relationships in international fora, and the struggles which were ongoing with the Greek Cypriot side.

A long life, a long friendship. Vamık Volkan, with his professional background, was in a good position to support the Denktaş family in what were often dark days and they grew very close.

Although the couple Rauf and Aydın Denktaş experienced many achievements and joys over certain periods of their lives, the pain of losing three of their children was abiding.

Vamık Volkan:

The worst situation a person might go through is the grief of losing a child. Rauf Denktaş and his wife Aydın lost three children. In 1957 they lost a daughter. A year later their second child, a boy, died while undergoing a tonsillectomy. In 1985 they would lose their firstborn son. The first of these losses happened in England. They don't even know where the grave of this child of theirs is. You need to understand this pain. I met them for the first time about forty years ago when Mrs. Denktaş called and invited me to the presidential palace. They had just moved in. I accepted the invitation and duly arrived to find that President Denktaş was so busy that he had no time to grieve. And Mrs. Denktaş didn't want to disturb him with her concerns. During this first visit I found out from Mrs. Denktaş, by virtue of my profession, that she kept somewhere some clothes of their child who had died in England in 1957 and that she occasionally took them out and looked at them. Her husband was unaware of this.

When Mrs. Denktaş felt the need to tell me this, I asked her to get the clothes and to share the experience with her husband.

When Mrs. Denktaş brought her deceased daughter's clothes into the room, the president finally realized what his wife had been doing. They cried as if this moment of such pain were new.

From this point, our friendship developed and lasted until he left us. I got involved in world affairs but I did not once trouble my presidential friend in this respect. And he never asked me if he should do this or that in politics. Our relationship was such.

It was not much later when the loss of another child compounded the couple's pain, an inconsolable grief. We routinely corresponded in the following years. I went frequently to the Denktaş home when I came to Cyprus. His door was always open to me. One day, when I was in the States, I got a call from Cyprus. "Vamık Volkan, come over, Mr. Rauf's son has died." This was their third loss. I was able to come over within a week, not sooner. When I did manage to get to Cyprus, I was sitting in front of my sister's house when a car pulled up and a window rolled down. It was Rauf Denktaş. He waved. I got into the car next to him. He didn't say anything. He was driving the car himself. We went to the graveyard together and sat in front of his son's grave for three hours. We didn't utter a single word. Friendship is sometimes something which is shared in silence.

It is very hard to evaluate history by today's lights. We need to evaluate people according to the time they lived in. When we look at it from this perspective, we see Rauf Denktaş as a man who identified himself with Atatürk. A man who dedicated himself to the affairs of Cyprus and who was determined to create a Turkish people whose father he would be.

His door was always open, as I say, and I stepped through it. Although I lived in the USA, Cyprus and Denktaş were always in my mind; I would mention him in my speeches on political psychology when I got the chance.

At times, the Denktaş couple visited Vamık and his family in the USA.

Rauf Denktaş came to visit us from time to time, to my great pleasure. At first, he would show up without much difficulty, but then responsibilities grew, as did his place in the world. Something was changing at the time of his last visit. At the small airport of the town I lived in where I always went to welcome him, the police took great security measures because Denktaş was coming. There were a lot of uniformed police officers and also plainclothes policemen. They didn't allow me to welcome him. He saw me by chance just as I was leaving the airport. He ordered the car to stop. "The world has changed a lot now, I can't visit you so easily anymore," he said.

Vamık Volkan corresponded with Rauf Denktaş for years. In this correspondence one can see the depth of their friendship; one can also see the course of history.

CHAPTER SIX

The Immortal Atatürk book

Mustafa Kemal Atatürk in 1925.

Vamık Volkan, with the Princeton University historian Norman Itzkowitz, has written a book in which he subjects Mustafa Kemal Atatürk, the founder of modern Turkey, to psychoanalytic examination (Volkan & Itzkowitz, 1984). No easy task. Not only because of the very complex subject matter, but also due to the impossibility of adopting a single approach to writing a psychoanalytic biography. Sigmund Freud followed various paths in his biographical works on Leonardo da Vinci and Moses (1910c, 1937b). The difficulty here seems greater, as Freud's two figures date far back and Moses is a semi-mythological figure. While admiring Freud's temerity at attempting this and also his couch-side manner in bringing out his subject, Leonardo, as a mild-mannered, sensitive genius, one cannot help thinking that a "final theory" is illusive, or perhaps impossible. With Moses, held to be a non-Jew by Freud's reckoning, this is all the more doomed an undertaking as there is little knowledge and little consensus on who he actually was. With Atatürk, this is not necessarily the case, for as challenging a project as it may be, psychoanalysing a very well-documented individual who existed within living memory should meet with more success.

There have been advances in theory and practice in the field of psychoanalysis of great figures from the past over the last hundred years or so. Focusing on artists, historical personalities, various geniuses in their numerous fields, several approaches have been adopted. To begin with artists, the earliest endeavors were to examine symbols, shapes, and forms of expression present in their works. An obvious example is the angularity of the cubists, the distortion of faces and bodies, and the highly unrealistic and stylized perceived reality of the environment of a given work. Conclusions could be drawn as to the psychological state of the artist through analysis of these paintings. Or could they? There was no attempt at the inception of this discipline to get at the driving force of the creativity of any given individual. The approach, therefore, came into question. As Martin S. Bergmann observes, "Symbols are overdetermined and their meaning is less constant and less universal than Freud assumed" (1973, p. 835).

Robert Waelder (1936), an Austrian psychoanalyst who studied under Anna Freud, begged to differ from the one-lane approach to this question and proposed a multifunctional approach in 1930. He posited that there were multiple conscious and unconscious meanings and impulses for the decisions, actions, and outcomes of a given subject. In other words, multiple determinants. This led writers in the field of psychoanalysis to extend their attention to political views, ideology, artistic expression, the world of work, and destructive behavior and violence. Research into child development sheds light on the importance of dual child–mother experiences in the formation of the self and the development of the ego of the child. Trauma suffered in childhood has a very great bearing on the life of the adult. For the writer of a biography, this is a factor which needs to be examined in order to comprehend the complex thing which is a human life. How ego is overdeveloped or underdeveloped, how the ego interacts with other mental factors, and what kind of defensive mechanisms or positive stimuli (praise, approval), are crucial factors to understand if we are to present a biography with some satisfaction.

When Erik Erikson (1958) applied his "theory of the stages of psychosocial development" to biography writing, the character of the psychoanalytic biography significantly changed. Erikson suggested that while approaching the relationship of the individual and society, the biography writer should focus more on the years of adolescence, that is, the time when an individual opens up to a wider societal circle beyond family and neighbors. As the person concerned progresses through life, the problems of young adulthood and the phenomenon of midlife crisis should also be taken into account by the biography writer.

One of the basic issues preoccupying psychoanalysts is a biographer's temptation to project his or her own desires, fantasies, and expectations (i.e. countertransference) onto the subject. Writers of biography may choose their subjects because they have an obsession with them, or because they feel especially close to them. To call a biography psychoanalytic, we have to know how the writer approaches the various aspects of countertransference. When the countertransferences are overlooked or left un-analysed, the depiction of the life in question is incomplete (Volkan, 2008).

Dr. Volkan's research into Atatürk was quite a task. To my question as to why he would want to undertake such a monumental work, he answered:

I understood as things went on that I was looking for an opportunity to get to know my father better by researching Atatürk.

The fact that Atatürk was also a replacement child was a factor in this endeavor. Dr. Volkan wanted to understand himself. Later, he also realized that by spending seven years examining Atatürk's life he was reviewing what he had left behind by coming to America. Dr. Volkan's research on Atatürk became an important work for his developing a healthy biculturalism as an immigrant.

Vamık Volkan and Norman Itzkowitz adopted a developmental approach while writing their biography of Kemal Atatürk (1984). Later, with Andrew

Dodd, they wrote the biography of Richard Nixon in concert (Volkan, Itzkowitz, & Dodd, 1997). After this collaborative work, Dr. Volkan undertook to write the life of Abdullah Öcalan (often known as Apo), leader of the Kurdistan Workers' Party (PKK/Partiya Karkeren Kürdistan) (Volkan,1997). This he wrote alone.

Their methodology is based on evidence presented chronologically. First one looks at infancy and childhood. This involves the bilateral relationship between the child and the mother. This includes the unconscious fantasies of the child, as well as of the mother and other carers; also, the environment of the child during the oedipal phase. The relevance here to the formation of the superego is of great importance in understanding the growing child. In adolescence, the individual tends to review his (the following is equally applicable to her) childhood; in other words, self-consciously examine his own psychology. As personality crystallizes, the individual goes through the life stages, adapting to his environment, trying to change his environment, attempting to meet his own demands, wishing to retain self-respect, dealing with sexual awakening, selecting a sexual partner. More often than not, the individual then has to adapt to the huge life change involved in parenting. Throughout adult life, the indvidual questions his changes in identity, regressions observed during the reinforcement of personality, and then the phenomenon of finding himself middle aged. And as we go on, there is reacting to the ageing process and to the approach of death. Thus, the life of the subject is examined through a psychoanalytic lens. Of course, the success of a psychoanalytic biography depends on the availability or paucity of information on the subject.

Writing about, or even talking about, Atatürk is a very sensitive issue in Turkey. He remains a giant figure in Turkish life and any criticism of the "father of the nation" can bring about instant retribution. There are laws in place forbidding any negative utterances concerning the man and his works. For this reason, books about him have tended to be written by non-Turks. Lord Kinross (1965) and Andrew Mango (2002) have both produced seminal works on Atatürk from the comfort of elsewhere. Nevertheless, Dr. Volkan pressed ahead with his and Itzkowitz's biography of the founder of the Turkish Republic, and, consequently, trouble started to brew. Extreme nationalists asserted that the book denigrated Atatürk. Dr. Volkan started to feel that visiting Turkey might not be prudent at this time. But were these attacks justified? Here is a look at the book, starting with a brief summary of Atatürk's life.

The founder of modern Turkey, Mustafa Kemal Atatürk, was born in Thessaloniki, a coastal town under Ottoman rule at the time (now in Greece). His father was a customs officer and a small-time businessman. He died when Mustafa was seven. In adolescence, Mustafa left home to attend cadet school. Although he thus became an army officer of the Ottoman military, he criticised the Sultan and he was active in organisations opposing the government.

During World War One, Mustafa Kemal saw active service at Gallipoli and due to his truly heroic defence of this vital position he became a general at the age of thirty-five.

Following WWI, the Allies threatened to carve up whatever was left of the Ottoman Empire. The Sultan was incapable of resisting the incursions of the British, French, Italians, Russians and Greeks. Mustafa Kemal set out to rescue the Turkish people and to ensure an independent future for the nation. Following the defeat of the Ottoman Empire at the end of the Great War, he left Istanbul for Anatolia. The Sultan, who had become anxious about his growing influence and who was under pressure from the Allies, ordered his dismissal from the army. In response, Mustafa Kemal formed a temporary national government and was duly elected its leader. Ankara at this time was a provincial city, yet now the hub of national resistance. Plans were laid to eject an invading Greek army from Anatolia and this is what transpired. Greece was conclusively defeated by 1922. The Sultan was deposed by the nationalist government and in 1923 the Turkish Republic was founded under the leadership of Mustafa Kemal.

When Mustafa Kemal became the first president of Turkey, he embarked on thorough and extensive political and cultural changes that would transform Turkey into a modern, secular, and westernised nation. He was given the surname Atatürk [father of the Turks]. Among the sea changes of these times were the abolition of Islamic law, secularisation in relation to the state and its functions, citizenship regulated on European models, enfranchisement of women, adoption of the Latin alphabet in place of Arabic script, and various economic reforms.

Most Turks will accept that Mustafa Kemal almost single-handedly rallied a war-weary nation to do battle for their independence and that he subsequently instituted a cultural revolution that helped to forge a modern state and a new national identity. He died in 1938, yet he has been seen as "the Immortal Leader" in Turkey ever since. His picture is iconic and ubiquitous and he will always be remembered as the founder of the new Turkey.

Mustafa, as we will call him now (he was later called Kemal—the word means clever in Turkish—by a teacher when he was ten or so and the name stuck) was born in the winter of 1880–1881, although the exact date of his advent is not known. His place of birth was Thessaloniki, perhaps in a pink three-story house which today is a museum. His sister, Makbule, however, asserted that he was in fact born in his paternal grandparents' house nearby (Aydemir, 1969, p. 484). At the time, Thessaloniki was an Ottoman town with a population of 80,000 or so and around half of the populace was Jewish. A quarter or so were Turkish, and the remainder were Greeks, Albanians, and Slavs.

Ali Rıza, Mustafa's father, was from an old Thessaloniki family, hailing originally from the Söke county of Aydın province. His father had a brush with the turbulent history of the region long before his grandson did. An incident on May 10, 1876 changed his life and not for the better. A young Christian Bulgarian girl named Stephana arrived in the city by train accompanied by her mother, and an imam decided to force the little girl to convert to Islam. The mother objected very strongly to this and screamed until some Greek Christians intervened and took the girl away from the imam, carrying her off to the American consulate. This provoked a protest by a number of Muslim Turks and blood was spilled, including that of the German and French consuls (Lewis, 1968). They were, in fact, beaten to death. Thereupon European warships appeared with the intention of forcing the arrest of the murderers and the other protestors. Ali Rıza's father was among the protestors and he thought it wise to take to the hills, literally. He spent the seven years before his death in the mountains of Macedonia.

A short while after his father's escape, Ali Rıza joined a group of volunteers who constituted a kind of national guard for the protection of Turkish interests at a time of high tension between the Ottoman Empire and Russia. He became a lieutenant, but then dropped out at the end of 1887 or early in 1878.

Seven or eight years before this brief military service, Ali Rıza had married a girl named Zübeyde who was fourteen or fifteen years old and twenty years his junior. Zübeyde settled into Ali Rıza's family's house in the Yeni Kapı neighborhood of Thessaloniki. She soon gave birth to three children—two boys, Ömer and Ahmet, and a girl, Fatma.

Ali Rıza became a customs officer in a desolate place called Pasha Bridge, 120 km from Thessaloniki. Pasha Bridge was a checkpoint on the border between the Ottoman Empire and Greece at this time and it was no easy matter to get back and forth from Thessaloniki. The young bride Zübeyde, now tending to three children and not yet twenty, lived with her husband's extended family and she saw her husband but seldom.

Fatma died in infancy, after which Zübeyde and the two boys moved to Pasha Bridge in spite of it being no place for civilized life. Tragedy stalked this young woman mercilessly. Her two sons also died. She lived, moreover, in constant fear of being abducted by Greek gangs from just over the border.

Ali Rıza formed a partnership with a lumber merchant called Cafer Efendi, took his wife back to Thessaloniki, presumably to her profound relief, and it was at this time that her third son was born, the Mustafa who would later be known as Atatürk.

Mustafa's birth coincided with a short period of economic well-being that the family experienced. Zűbeyde gave birth to two more children, but only Mustafa and his sister Makbule survived. When Mustafa was seven, his father, whose business had not been going very well for a few years (the forest used for the local lumber trade was burned down by Greek bandits), probably sank into depression, took to drink, and died. Zűbeyde was widowed at twenty-seven.

It could be said that Mustafa was born into a "house of the dead" (Volkan & Itzkowitz, 1984, 2011). According to what his sister Makbule later recounted, when she and Mustafa were kids, their dead little siblings would be discussed at home, along with the vile life at the Ottoman–Greek border, riddled with bandits. With the pain of loss, with one death after another, Zübeyde turned to God. She became known as "Mullah" (the pious one). Yet she also tried to appear a merry widow, dressing well and hiding her grief, behaving as a headstrong woman and pooh-poohing formality. But the religious side of her was deep. Her family were Hacı Sufis, Muslims with a strong inclination towards mysticism.

Shortly before his death, Mustafa's father gave him a gift (Volkan & Itzkowitz, 1984, 2011): secularism. Mustafa Kemal imparted this to the journalist Ahmet Emin Yalman (Emin, 1922) as one of his first memories. Zübeyde wanted Mustafa to be enrolled in a religious school in the near vicinity of the family home. Here he would memorize the entire Quran and be prepared for the life of an imam. Ali Rıza had other ideas. He wanted his remaining son to be educated in a modern manner and on secular principles. A young man named Şemsi Efendi had started a school in Thessaloniki around that time and Ali Rıza was determined to send Mustafa there. First Mustafa attended the religious school for a few days.

Then Ali Rıza enrolled his son in Şemsi Efendi's school. After his father died, for economic reasons, the family moved 30 kilometers away to live with a relative in a rural area. Sometime later his mother sent Mustafa back to Thessaloniki in order for him to continue his education. Atatürk recalled that this relative was a *teyze* (an aunt). One day the boy was beaten by a sadistic teacher, one Kaymak Hafiz Efendi, a man known for his firm religious convictions. "My whole body was covered in blood," he later recounted (Emin, 1922).

Zübeyde remarried and this enraged the adolescent Mustafa. Indeed, we could see this as a traumatic event coming on top of his loss of his beloved father. As he progressed from primary school to cadet school, the teenage Mustafa touched home base more and more infrequently. This may have had a bearing on his setting his face firmly towards secularism and the modernization that was to be the hallmark of his later rule of his country.

It was at cadet school that Mustafa earned his second name, Kemal. He shone at mathematics and for this reason his teacher gave him this soubriquet. It means something between clever and perfect. The name Kemal all but replaced his given name of Mustafa.

Vamık Volkan contends that the mind of the young Mustafa Kemal was greatly influenced by his mother's grief on the micro scale and the desperate plight of his nation on the macro. From these sadnesses and difficulties came a determination to change the polity, to westernize and to embrace a new secular approach to the way society was to be run. Key to this latter aspiration was the abolition of the caliphate. As well as the abolition of the Sublime Porte (Ottoman central government).

Dr. Volkan ascribes much of the impulses involved in this great undertaking to Mustafa Kemal's earliest memories. His desire to please his mother and to follow his father is most important here. Love and care for the former, the religious and traditionally minded mother and emulation of the latter, the more modern and secular-minded father. His elementary school teacher Şemsi Efendi must also have been an influential role model, with his penchant for the emerging modern world.

When Mustafa Kemal was head of state and ensconced in his presidential palace, his mother lived with him. He developed a daily ritual in regard to her. Of a morning he would rise and visit her room, kiss her in the traditional, rather mechanical way, and then turn his attention to affairs of state. Zübeyde died on January 14, 1924. Mustafa Kemal visited her grave for the first time on January 27 and made a speech there. This speech is telling insofar as it reveals a link between his image of his mother and his desire to engineer the deliverance of his country:

> I am, needless to say, deeply saddened by my mother's death. Yet, there is something that negates my sorrow and consoles me. This something is to know that the administration which brought our mother the country to destruction and ruin has gone to the grave of oblivion, never again to return. (Atatürk, 1952, vol. 2, pp. 74–75)

The Immortal Atatürk presents the reader with a psychoanalytic examination of the life of a political leader and explores his motivation for creating a nation. This could be a guide for future works on this subject. With Dr. Volkan's permission we can now take a look at some of the contents. We may also reflect on the vacuity of some of Dr. Volkan's detractors in regard to this work. Yet there should be a caveat here. Despite all the research Volkan and Itzkowitz carried out, there is a scarcity of information about Mustafa's childhood, schooling, and teenage years. As noted already, we do not even know his exact date of birth. The one sibling who survived him, Makbule, left memoirs which Volkan and Itzkowitz examined, but these are not comprehensive by any means. One thing that they yield, however, is that one of Mustafa's siblings was buried in a grave either on the seaside or in a riverbed. When the water rose, the body rose too and it was then found— having been partially devoured by animals.

Other primary sources were sifted and the two writers garnered as much information as they could from families with a history intertwined with Atatürk's and a certain amount of useful data emerged.

Whether this data is accurate or not and whether the story of the brother's burial is historical fact, is a matter for conjecture and future study. What we can say is that Mustafa Kemal faced grief and anguish from an early age and that the causes of grief must have seemed interminable. Dr. Volkan had this to say:

> Psychoanalysts often encounter parents who go through complicated mourning experiences, for example, those who have lost their children. After a woman has lost her child, she knowingly or unknowingly becomes concerned as to whether her next child, should she give birth again, will survive. In a sense, the next arrival replaces the dead child and this new child becomes a psychological

> link with the one that has gone. The existing child is identified with the dead child (that he or she has, of course, never met) in the mind of the mother, with profound consequences for the surviving child's forming identity.

The mother concerned may well be rather strict with her surviving child and perhaps a little distant. She may see her child as representing her sense of loss and she may fear that he or she will go the same way. As the mother and the child interact, the things the mother "transfers" to the child and her perception of this child as a replacement, will affect him or her deeply. Psychoanalysts have observed that it is possible that a child in such a relationship might fantasize about ridding his or her mother of grief (Volkan & Itzkowitz, 1984, 2011). Such fantasies tend to revolve around the mother ceasing to focus on a dead child (or husband) and thereby giving sufficient love and attention to the living child. Such a child may be highly preoccupied with the mother's virtues and this can continue into adulthood. She becomes a symbolic representation of virtue.

Dr. Volkan speculates that due to his siblings' early deaths, the young Mustafa might have had fantasies of becoming a kind of savior and a savior who was a living connection to his dead siblings. He also speculates that the impulse to rescue his country from utter ruin, and to provide succor to those turned into refugees by the Balkan Wars and the Great War, found its gestation in his very early years. Attempting to prove his hypothesis that these pre-oedipal preoccupations affected Mustafa's life, Dr. Volkan sifted the evidence and found it.

What we know regarding what Mustafa remembers about this period reflects the struggle between his mother and his father concerning how Mustafa should be permitted to progress and how his father prevailed. Yet, it is known that his father compromised by allowing his son to complete his entry procedures to the religious school with a ceremony a few days before he started at Ali Rıza's preferred progressive school. Dr. Volkan contends that Mustafa revered his father partly because of his antipathy towards Islamic tradition and his reservations about the state of the Ottoman Empire. This reverence was partly a factor in opposing his mother. Memory is shifting sand and young Mustafa recalls his father's time as a customs officer, when in fact this phase of Ali Rıza's career had ceased long before this supposed recollection. What was not recalled, or admitted, was the image of

Mustafa's father as an unsuccessful and ailing man. This, Dr. Volkan argues, was suppressed, and, indeed, denied. Dr. Volkan elaborates:

> Clinical studies show how important it is for a child to replace a father who dies at a child's oedipal period with someone else, so we were curious as to whether this void in young Mustafa might have been filled by Şemsi Efendi. Non-religious education reached the first schools in large cities at this time and pious Muslim Turks strongly objected. Şemsi Efendi's school was attacked twice, its classrooms ransacked, but he was undeterred from pursuing modern education. We developed the hypothesis that Mustafa substituted his teacher, a progressive and decisive man who was similar to his own father's idealized image, for his father. We put into a theoretical framework the idea that his idealization of these two men was a significant factor in his appreciation of things Western and his determination to modernize Turkey. And we started to speculate that the Sultan, whom Mustafa Kemal would come to see as weak and corrupt, might have represented his father's character weaknesses.
>
> What is known about Mustafa Kemal's adolescence shows that this period is marked by struggles for separation–individuation where he tries to distinguish himself from his mother (or her mental representation). In the theoretical framework, we determined that Mustafa's oedipal "victory"—his loss of his "rival" for his mother's love upon his father's death—had rendered the mother–son relationship problematic and full of uncertainties. He was there for his mother at this difficult time and he was the connection to her dead children; yet, on the other hand, this could have been psychologically suffocating for his mother who was in a state of chronic grief.

After his father's death, Mustafa and his sisters lived in a smallholding outside Thessaloniki with their mother. Mustafa soon returned to the city to stay with one of his relatives. He coveted the uniforms of the boys who went to cadet school and decided to take up a military education. Even though Zübeyde had respect for the military, she strongly objected to Mustafa Kemal's choice to become a soldier. He took the cadet school exams on his own initiative, unbeknownst to her. It was all presented to his mother as a fait accompli.

As has been stated, Mustafa Kemal was angry about his mother's remarriage. As soon as the nuptials were over, he packed his bags and left home for the military academy in Bitola (today in Macedonia, about 150 kilometres from Thessaloniki), and there he took up residence, not returning to his mother's home for some years. Dr. Volkan believes that Mustafa's personality formation throughout childhood and adolescence involved a large element of self-sufficiency. One can speculate that this character facet was fostered by living in what could be seen as a kind of "house of death," and by his conflict with his mother.

Joining the army meant joining the most westernized institution in the Ottoman Empire. It was run to a great extent on German lines and the uniforms were to an extent European in character. Here Mustafa Kemal found himself in a situation much more to his late father's liking and in opposition to his mother's ideal milieu for her son.

Thereby leaving mourning and religion behind, Mustafa Kemal entered adulthood in a way of his own choosing. And this seminal choice was, in Volkan's and Itzkowitz's opinion, to have long-lasting consequences, not only for the man himself, but also for Turkey, and not simply in relation to war and politics (in the strict sense). When he assumed the presidency, Mustafa Kemal decided upon Ankara as the new capital of the new polity. This, historians tend to agree, was in order to underline the fresh start of the new nation and to escape the massive baggage of history that Istanbul entailed. Mustafa Kemal, later Atatürk, wished to make Ankara a "house of life" in the late 1920s and the early 1930s. He wanted to see the brilliant spirit of Berlin and Paris in his new capital city, still rather provincial though it was. He encouraged music, dancing, colorful ballrooms, and all other manner of entertainment. He had adopted a young boy during the war and now he began adopting girls. His purpose was clear—to bring up females in the new Western style and to encourage them to achieve excellence in their own right.

One of these girls became very famous—Sabiha Gökçen. The second airport of Istanbul is named after her, most appropriately since she became an aviator in what was almost completely a man's field worldwide. Amelia Earhart and Amy Johnson are remembered as the female exceptions which prove the rule. Sabiha was the most prominent flyer in Turkey in her day.

Sabiha Gökçen, who was around sixty at the time, recounted to Dr. Volkan that Atatürk forbade his subordinates to indulge in any expression of mourning. He more or less ordered his adopted daughters to laugh, to make merry. Indeed, Sabiha Gökçen recalls, he told them not to trust anyone who did not laugh.

His adopted children were not to be raised in the manner his mother had practiced. There was to be no denial of compassion, no strict religious observance, no atmosphere of oppression and gloom. As Mustafa Kemal's mother had turned to religion for solace in a time of mourning, her son exhibited a commensurate rejection of mourning and faith, particularly in relation to what he saw as its pernicious effects on politics and social progress. During his presidency, Atatürk shut down dervish lodges (Islamic monasteries) and opposed those who publicly revered Islamic saints, contending that what they were doing was a form of idolatry. He believed that appealing to the dead is a blemish on a civilized society (Afetinan, 1971).

Following the collapse of the Ottoman Empire, Istanbul was under occupation in the form of the forces of the victorious Allied powers. Mustafa Kemal had resolved to leave the city and raise the country in an effort to rid her of foreign troops in what was to become the War of Deliverance. The night before his departure, he had dinner with his mother. He donned Ottoman garb and sat on the floor to eat in the Islamic manner. He was never seen in public in such clothes, but to please his mother he conformed on this night to her traditions and wishes. This was part of a pattern. Just as he had attended the opening ceremony of his mother's preferred (religious) school and then headed for his father's preferred (non-religious) school, so now he gave his mother an evening in her preferred way, then departed to undertake things she could hardly imagine and in the most modern manner. He told her he was leaving and she prayed for him.

The following day he set out on his perilous journey to raise the standard and to attempt to save the Turks from national oblivion.

Throughout the war, Mustafa Kemal stuck to this relationship pattern with his mother and he continued to do so during his presidency. The ritual was the same. He would approach her respectfully, kiss her hand in the traditional way, and then revert to modern forms of behavior.

Being "tested" and admitted to the modern world of the army can be seen as a symbol of his intrapsychic separation from his mother's mental representation, and one can see this situation repeat itself as his life progressed.

Atatürk said in 1921, "Freedom and liberty are my character." He had been possessed by a love of freedom since childhood. He added,

I also take it as an essential condition that my nation must have the same qualities. To be able to live, I must remain the son of a sovereign state. For this reason, I hold national independence to be a matter of life and death. (Aydemir, 1969, vol. 1, p. 484)

Dr. Volkan believes that these utterances point to the melding of his personal and public life.

Since my childhood, in my home, I have not liked being together with either my mother or sister, or a friend. I have always preferred to be alone and independent, and have lived this way always. ... Because when one is given advice one has either to accept and obey it—or disregard it altogether. Neither response seems right to me. Wouldn't it be a regressive retreat to the past to heed a warning given to me by my mother who is more than 20 or 25 years older than I? Yet were I to rebel against it I would break the heart of my mother, in whose virtue and lofty womanhood I have the firmest belief. (Aydemir, 1969, vol. 1, p. 484)

Şemsi Efendi died in 1917. Deriving from the Arabic word Şems, meaning the sun, the name Şemsi means "illuminator," which is an appropriate name for a teacher. The sun was an important symbol for Atatürk throughout his life. The image often found its way into his speeches as a symbol of saving his troubled country from darkness. Interestingly, many followers of Atatürk saw him as the symbol of a sun that would bring a new light to Turkey by scattering the black clouds floating over the shattered Ottoman Empire. Journalists in his time even referred to him as the "Saviour Sun." Some who met him for the first time said they could not meet his eyes due to their gleaming blue and the aura that this generated. Volkan and Itzkowitz find in this a symbol of hope and regeneration, a reflection of light that Mustafa wished would dispel the darkness surrounding his mother in her state of perpetual mourning. And in order to take this a little deeper, they decided to look into Atatürk's unconscious.

Dr. Volkan states that dreams are important in the psychoanalytic process, as are daydreams. Yet, there is only one recorded dream of Atatürk's. This dream is a premonition of his mother's death soon after the War of Deliverance. His mother was in Izmir on the day she died. And Mustafa Kemal was in Ankara. When he woke that morning, they handed him a telegram. He said he knew what was written in the telegram. We do not, however, have any details of this dream, rendering a psychological biographer's task rather difficult in this respect. Volkan and Itzkowitz had to look for other symbolic references.

One such reference arises from an article by Atatürk. The subject is the relationship of man with nature and it contains important clues:

> Coming or not coming into the world is not in man's gift. As soon as and after man comes into the world he is inferior to nature and many creatures. He requires protection, feeding, care and guidance. (Afetinan, 1971, pp. 77–78)

Vamık Volkan:

This statement brings to mind the story of Mustafa's brother who was buried near the sea or in a river bank and then ripped to pieces by wild animals. Man is born at a tender stage of development, at the mercy of nature, at the mercy of his fellow creatures. Atatürk's words seem to my mind to be a personal undertaking to be the ideal father. He protected his country when at war, tried to feed her through agricultural reforms, and was a "teacher" to the Turkish people. I can say he has become the idealized father of the Turks over time through the transformation of the nation.

I am a Cypriot Turk. Atatürk was the idol of my people and he was a part of my idealized self as I grew up. As everyone in Turkey can see due to the myriad portraits, statues, and monuments they come across, "Ata Türk" (literally, Father of the Turks) seems superhuman. While trying to piece together the information I gathered into a realistic picture, it was rather hard to find the point of balance between the human and superhuman aspects of my subject. While working on the book, I was often reminded of how my father courageously identified with Atatürk (of whom there was much talk in our family) when he banned the fez and introduced the Western-style hat. When he promoted Western hats, Turkish men submissively threw away their fezzes and went about trying to find themselves a hat. And my father, imitating Atatürk, went into a coffee house in a conservative Cypriot Turkish village with a Western hat on and stepped onto a stool to demonstrate the change. However, unlike Atatürk, my father's courage was met only with hostility by the armed villagers. At least for a while.

Throughout my childhood, I listened to this story of my father's many times and I thought my father had failed—unlike Atatürk. But after examining Atatürk's life at large, I began to appreciate my father's courage. I have actually given up my childhood's godlike image of Atatürk in my mind. He is, after all, similar to numerous other people who have been through a troubled childhood. A dream I had about Atatürk once led me to better understand my own countertransference. In my dream, Atatürk and a patient I was seeing at that time had swapped identities. My young patient was handsome and talented like Atatürk and I had the thought that he was the Last Renaissance Man. Both of them had very a high sense of self, indeed, a particular thing Atatürk said might have come out of my patient's mouth.

> Why would I stoop to the level of the common people after becoming a highly educated person over all these years, after learning to take pleasure in freedom, after analyzing modern life and society? I will lift them up to my level. Let them be like me, not me like them! (Aydemir, 1969, vol. 3, p. 482)

There were reasons originating from childhood for both of them to develop an exaggerated sense of self. They had both been through terrible losses at a young age, they had both had to mature at an early age, they had both regarded themselves as "number one" and strived to gain approval for this. Despite not having had a strong bond with their mothers, in both cases the mother saw her son as a potential "savior" and supported his development of a high sense of self.

One of the differences between Dr. Volkan's patient and Atatürk was that while his patient's exaggerated narcissism led him over time to turn to psychoanalysis, the other decided to become the leader of his country. However, the similarities were there. Each led Dr. Volkan to understand more about the other. The greatness of Atatürk lay in the fact that he actualized his own internal expectations and requirements. As his struggle turned into Turkey's struggle, his narcissistic needs changed and he too changed.

The Immortal Atatürk, as a psychological biography of a leader, has attracted great attention worldwide. The attention it gained in Turkey on the release of the first edition was not all as positive as might be wished. Dr. Volkan:

> Although I understand the sensitivity of the issue, it is not easy to understand the reaction to the fact that Atatürk too was a human being.

As already suggested, writing a psychological biography, especially for someone many years dead, is not a simple thing. On completion, Dr. Volkan noticed that Professor Itzkowitz was moved to tears. On publication of the book, Dr. Norman Knorr, Dean of the University of Virginia School of Medicine, held a celebratory reception. This was an event Dr. Volkan and his wife attended with great pleasure. It was also the evening that he let go of Atatürk. That night he had a dream. He saw newspapers in many languages announcing Atatürk's death. This was a dream steeped in sadness. It was time to let Atatürk rest in peace and to move on.

Despite restrictions on the publication of the book, it hit the shelves in Turkey a few months after appearing in the United States. Vamık Volkan sent a copy to Rauf Denktaş, who read it in one night. Denktaş did not necessarily know much about the incubation of the work, but he understood. The following day he sent a letter to Kenan Evren, head of Turkey's armed forces and now president of the Republic following a coup. In his letter, he wrote that the supposedly offending book actually had the great value of portraying Atatürk as a human being, that it was a means to understanding his nature on a deeper level. Opposition to the work largely melted away.

Denktaş wrote to Vamık Volkan:

> Dear Vamık
>
> Thank you for *The Immortal Atatürk*. While waiting for Mr. Kyprianou, who will return to New York after receiving his instructions from Greece, I devoured the book! To my generation, Atatürk is faultless, like a god. With the passage of time his message to the Turkish people seems not only immortal but more immediate than ever. I did have a slight fear when we discussed your project that your psychoanalytic approach might have harmed the man's immortal legacy. On the contrary. I am happy to tell you that thanks to your book I have faced his mortality. As with everybody else, he,

too, was affected in his childhood, youth and throughout his entire career by daily events, hardships, disasters, deficiencies, desires and passions. Therefore, his achievements gain a still greater meaning and magnificence. His immortality is as a leader and the creator of a nation. He himself was a mortal who achieved the impossible; he became a guide in the history of nations struggling for freedom and justice. It was a great experience for me to discover that Atatürk was a human. Thank you, congratulations and I am glad to have you as a friend.

R. R. Denktaş

The Immortal Atatürk has also been translated into Japanese and Greek, gaining wide attention. The hostility has evaporated.

We too can now let Atatürk rest under a Turkish sky and move on.

CHAPTER SEVEN

Psychoanalytical practices: "What does Dr. Volkan treat?"

A lot of people have been on Dr. Volkan's couch. This part of the book concentrates on the concept of personality organizations and particular case studies that exemplify the four personality organizations that analysts encounter most often. (Cases described in this chapter were first presented by Dr. Volkan: June 12–13, 2015: Seminars on psychoanalytic technique and case presentations. Istanbul Psychoanalytic Education, Research and Development Association (PSIKE), Istanbul, Turkey.) The phenomena examined in this chapter will undoubtedly be universal and applicable worldwide.

Personality organizations

The importance of the harmony between a baby and her (or equally his) mother in the development of mental image skills has been the subject of research, most particularly since the 1970s. For example, Bloom, 2010; Brazelton & Greenspan, 2000; Emde, 1991; Greenspan, 1981; Lehtonen, 2003, 2016; Purhonen et al., 2005; Stern, 1985.

One fact which has emerged is that the mind of a baby is far more active than researchers had previously believed. Nevertheless, a baby cannot really differentiate herself from others before emerging from early infancy. Dr. Volkan characterizes the mind of a baby as being in a state of creative confusion. Much has been learned about how a child develops the ability to psychologically separate herself from others and distinguish internalized or external objects from one another.

As Daniel Stern (1985) states, a baby is fed four to six times a day and each feeding experience brings about different degrees of pleasure. For this reason, Stern has it that as the baby develops, experiences are classified as "good" or "bad." Later, the child develops an ego function that allows her to bring together and to integrate an opposite self and external or internalized object images previously separated. After the child develops the ability to integrate, she becomes aware of the fact that her good and bad feelings are directed at the same target.

While evaluating the personality organization of an individual who seeks psychoanalysis, Dr. Volkan considers the two ego functions mentioned above—the ability to differentiate and the ability to integrate. Until the child reaches an important crossroads at which she starts to integrate opposite self and object images, there is a developmental compartmentalization in her mind that stores the good and bad images separately. The child who cannot integrate opposing images to some extent turns this developmental splitting into a defensive one and as an adult, in a sense, divides her self or objects into good and bad categories (see also Kernberg, 1980).

Vamık Volkan states that there are four personality organizations that analysts are generally familiar with. These are:

1. Neurotic
2. Narcissistic
3. Borderline
4. Psychotic.

A person who has the first personality organization can differentiate her self images from her external and internalized object images. She also differentiates one object image from another one. Furthermore, she integrates her self and object images.

Those who have the second and the third personality organization can differentiate to varying degrees, but cannot integrate to different degrees. The defensive separation, technically called "splitting," kicks in. These patients have disorders of the self because it is not fully integrated.

The person who has a psychotic personality organization is mostly unable to differentiate or integrate. Such a patient has a serious disorder of the self.

While evaluating the mental state of a person, Dr. Volkan started to ask himself, "What am I treating?" He looked beyond allocating the patient into a diagnostic category and instead started to address the indications of the disorder. To render intrapsychic conflicts more understandable, one needs to produce an "internal map" of the person and attempt to relate to it. Treatment means changing the individual's internal map to some degree— ideally, to a large degree. This change needs to be engineered under clinical observation with the patient starting to perform the psychological functions which he or she was previously unable to perform effectively.

Individuals with neurotic personality organization perceive their object and self-images realistically. They are able to have love and hate for the same person, thing, or situation. They experience anxiety as a signal of internal mental conflicts, which are primarily related to oedipal issues. According to Dr. Volkan, the pre-oedipal problems emerging during the psychoanalytic treatment of people with neurotic personality organization occur due to defensive regressions and a fixation on psychological progress rather than ego deficiencies. During their psychoanalysis such patients work out within themselves their oedipal issues.

According to Dr. Volkan, someone with a narcissistic personality organization differentiates his "grandiose self" (being number one, superior, fantastic) from his undervalued "hungry self." To visualize this, Dr. Volkan suggests imagining a pecan pie on a plate. A small piece is cut off and separated from the rest of this pie. The bigger part is sweet and appetizing. The smaller piece is not; someone has spilled vinegar on it. The two parts are not touching. A person with the disorder in question takes the larger piece and idealizes it and imagines it as "number one" while attempting to deny the existence of the "bad" (technically called "hungry"—hungry for love) self. A person with narcissistic personality organization also keeps the images of her external and internalized objects divided. She experiences the "good" others as those who adore her and who are separated from the devalued ("bad") ones.

In order to explain the self-representation of a person with a borderline personality organization, imagine a cake on a plate cut down the middle. One side is good and the other side is bad. Such individuals also perceive their objects as either good or bad.

People with psychotic personality organization have a fragmented self. They also have fragmented object images. Often, they cannot keep object images stable, they keep internalizing and externalizing them. Since they do not have a fully developed ego ability to differentiate, they cannot test reality and in their mind one fragmented element can be fused with another.

In order to illustrate the above technical concepts, there follow some brief case studies that relate to the aforementioned four types of personality organization. As can be seen, transference neurosis in someone with a neurotic personality organization will eventually need to face oedipal conflicts. Patients with the second and third personality organizations during their treatment first need to turn their internal structure towards neurotic personal organization after developing integration functions. They, too, must then examine oedipal problems. However, they act like a "normal" child entering the oedipal phase. It is as if it is the first time they have faced an oedipal situation and experienced an integrated self and integrated object representations. The treatment of individuals with psychotic personality organization focuses on helping such individuals to develop both differentiating and integrating ego functions.

Neurotic personality organization—a case study

A doctor in his mid-thirties, a man with an obsessive character, George, decided on analysis due to the confusion and distress he was experiencing in the wake of his wife walking out on him. In the analytical process it became clear both to Dr. Volkan and his patient that he had been a complete slave to his wife over the course of their seven-year marriage. He had bent over backwards to please her, buying her gifts he could ill afford, washing the dishes and taking out the trash, although he had little time for such things, and massaging her back to lull her to sleep to the point where his hands hurt. Dr. Volkan came to realize that beneath this submissive behavior, his patient was trying to deny his dependence on his wife and harbored quite a strong hostility toward her. His wife not only became tired of his servility, she also sensed his hostility and left him.

George's mother was an adopted child who clung to the fantasy that she was born into a noble family. When George was born, she passed this fantasy on to her child and expected him to actualize her own fantasies by achieving fame. To some extent this explains the son's acting like a slave to satisfy women and his perpetual anger towards them.

Childhood's long shadow has much to do with this. When he reached the oedipal stage, George's already highly charged relationship with his mother ratcheted up. His mother had the habit of leaving her husband's bed at night and wandering around the house from one room to another and from one bed to another. This awakened in the boy fantasies of laying claim to his mother and opposing his father, next to whom he felt belittled. The growing boy was taking a secret pride in the fact that he might surpass his father as a man and that his mother would consequently love him more than she loved her husband. Yet, because he had these kinds of oedipal–incestuous desires, he also feared that he might be punished by his father. His father often beat little George because of his habit of offending his mother. This reinforced the boy's desire to be independent of his mother. George had to submit to his father and take the beatings.

George grew up and got married. His father died of cancer soon after his son's wedding. While his father was experiencing his last painful moments, George did something interesting—he had sex in a room directly below that of his father. While he was making love to his wife, he knew very well that his father was drawing his last breath upstairs. Under analysis, George came to understand that his desire to have sex with his wife at the point of his father's death was primarily to show the dying father that his son now had his own wife and had no longer an interest in his father's wife, George's mother. On one level, this was a wish to magic away his oedipal conflict with his father's demise. On another, it was a way of telling the old man, "See? I have my own woman and you have your own woman. Each of us is with his wife. There is no need for competition, murder, or castration."

At the start of his third year of analysis, George's epiphany led him to feel closer to the mental image of his father. Consequently, he could now mourn for him. As the third year of analysis progressed, George was able to grapple with his disorder in all its severity and he managed to develop a transference neurosis in its fullest sense. In relation to this transference, Dr. Volkan was the oedipal father figure.

The patient got into a relationship with another psychiatrist's secretary. George saw this other psychiatrist a few times in his dreams and he was sporting a moustache. The other psychiatrist did not have a moustache, but Dr. Volkan did. George was merging them into a single image. For George, his psychoanalyst (Dr. Volkan), the other psychiatrist, and the secretary represented the three oedipal characters. Without saying anything, Dr. Volkan waited for the transference to become a workable transference neurosis.

The patient ended his relationship with the secretary and at the same time began to openly belittle Dr. Volkan during his sessions with him while simultaneously starting to fear him. Dr. Volkan again remained silent on these developments.

The patient later developed a certain ritual in Dr. Volkan's office. Every time he came for a session, he sat on the couch and removed his contact lenses before lying down, and upon rising to go he put his lenses back in. In a sense, he was symbolically removing his eyes in Dr. Volkan's presence, an act of self-castration, so that Dr. Volkan could not do this to the already-castrated George. Because he had "stolen" a psychiatrist's woman, the man's secretary, his anxiety in relation to castration had increased to the point that he dreamt of attacking another psychiatrist, a representation of Dr. Volkan, which resulted in a damaged cornea because he had forgotten to remove his contact lenses. After the violent dream, George was quite anxious on the couch and Dr. Volkan told him, without using technical terms, what he made of this ritual, that is, it was an oedipal transference neurosis which had flared up between them.

George duly renounced his lens ritual in light of what Dr. Volkan had told him and instead started to have fantasies about a miracle cure for his poor eyesight. Or, more likely, fantasizing about his castration issues vanishing.

Oedipal conflicts persisted between patient and analyst. The patient asked Dr. Volkan to hypnotize him in order to "open his memory box." He wanted Dr. Volkan to "get inside him" and developed the notion that his analyst had a curved penis. It seems George saw Dr. Volkan as a terrifying Turk who cut heads off with the traditional Turkish curved sword. After that he went pale on the couch, shaking with anxiety. He reflected that he too had a curved penis and some weeks later he decided Dr. Volkan's was in an S-shape. To him "S" could mean "snake," "S" could mean "shit."

George recalled that as a child he had defecated in the living room and had eaten the feces of the family dog. He recounted these events with a mixture of astonishment, fear, and joy. "Shit is strong," he explained. Dr. Volkan asked him to think over the idea that if he ate the bodily matter or parts of someone else, he could steal their qualities, such as the other's strength. This led him on to oral sex fantasies and he realized he wished to eat Dr. Volkan's penis. He came out with this fantasy on the couch, again shaking with anxiety. Dr. Volkan, for his part, mostly remained silent, allowing George to experience and to own up to his castration anxiety.

In the course of time, George was able to say "good" things about his father and accept his anger towards his mother, who had prevented him from having a close relationship with his father. He gradually became more positive towards Dr. Volkan. He was able to work on his Oedipus complex in depth. Dr. Volkan notes:

> There is nothing unusual in this example for experienced analysts. What George did can be easily explained by the classical definition of transference and transference neurosis and its resolution.

Narcissistic personality organization case study

Brown was thirty years old when he started psychoanalysis. He was a man who saw himself as the center of the universe and believed himself to be superior to others. He had a wife, a son, and two daughters. While his wife was giving birth to their third child, the boy, some problems arose in relation to the baby's health. It looked possible that the child might not grow up physically "perfect." Now, one of Brown's ancestors was a Founding Father of the United States and Brown, with this in mind, thought a feeble son would cast a negative shadow on what he considered an elite family. Brown's self-esteem was under threat. A short while after the birth Brown seduced a secretary, the daughter of a judge, who was working in her father's office. At that time, Brown's father, a lawyer, was the head of a prominent law firm and Brown was working in his father's office. Brown claimed that his fling with the judge's daughter was a great love affair. The girl got pregnant, had an abortion, and the affair ended. Brown ended up in Dr. Volkan's office seeking therapy.

On a superficial level, Brown's relationship with the judge's daughter was related to oedipal conflicts. Dr. Volkan explains:

> What comes to mind might be this. Having a "defective" child, in a sense, injured Brown's manhood and evoked Brown's castration anxiety and he seduced a woman "belonging" to his father/the judge in order to achieve an oedipal victory. The woman represented the mother figure. Paradoxically or not, the attempt at oedipal victory and the woman's abortion increased Brown's castration anxiety.

As analysis got under way, Dr. Volkan came to understand that oedipal matters were not active in Brown's mind. He considered that addressing these issues at the outset would not be helpful. Brown's primary concern was to protect his inner image of himself, known as the "grandiose self"

(Kernberg, 1975; Kohut, 1971; Volkan, 1976). Having a "defective" child was a blow to this grandiose self and he chose a "low status" lover to re-establish it. Comparing himself with this lover would prove that he was a superior being.

During the second year of analysis, Dr. Volkan learned that the judge's daughter was an individual with a lot of personal problems and flaws. She was unattractive and she was a kleptomaniac. A tumor in her stomach had been removed leaving ugly scars. She had undergone such severe problems with her teeth that they had all been removed and she wore dentures.

Vamık Volkan:

> The fact that she removed her dentures when she went down on Brown might be considered to ease Brown's vagina dentata (fear of a vagina having teeth to harm the male organ—i.e. fear of castration). Clinical studies show that some boys have fantasies of vagina dentata. When Brown told me about his girlfriend, what came to my mind first was the possibility that he had a vagina dentata fantasy. However, for the first years of analysis, Brown's main focus had not been on psychosexual matters. He used this woman to feed his grandiose self. Throughout the affair, he was always physically and mentally comparing himself to his lover and he felt he was easily the superior one. His lover helped him to regain his grandiose self.

On commencing analysis, Brown spoke in a monotone. His first apparent transference indicator appeared a few weeks after analysis had started. On a trip somewhere he seduced a "foreign woman" who spoke English with the accent of a non-native speaker. Dr. Volkan is also a non-native speaker and he retains his Turkish-influenced accent. So he is, in terms of subtle signals, a "foreigner," like the woman in question. Brown had sex with the woman in a manner that precluded intimacy and which involved a certain contempt for her.

Over the first years of analysis, Dr. Volkan discovered that there were various factors in Brown's childhood which led to his narcissistic organization. His father was distant and his mother was cold. His mother denied him adequate love while impressing upon him how special his family was.

Brown attempted to explain his narcissistic transference to Dr. Volkan by describing his preoccupation with Oliphant cartoons. These are black and white sketches of, generally, the rich and powerful. They also feature tiny human figures in juxtaposition with the huge rendering of the main subject. Brown told Dr. Volkan that he identified his devalued analyst with the tiny figures. Brown was not speaking of these characters as influential at this time. He was referring to their being tiny and unimportant.

Dr. Volkan learned that every day Brown would have many fantasies. Over time, Brown gave names to his fantasies, both those in daily life and also the fantasies of the bedroom. He gave his fantasies such epithets as "iron ball," "generous woman," and "the raped girl." He would lie on Dr. Volkan's couch and say that he'd had or was having a particular fantasy. The "iron ball" fantasy was a quite typical "glass bubble" fantasy in which a patient with narcissistic personality organization is alone in an extraordinary kingdom, with the lesser people shut out (Volkan, 1973). This is a manifestation of a grandiose self. In short, the patient places his grandiose self in a glass bubble and keeps everyone who represents his "hungry self" outside. Brown placed his grandiose self in an iron ball and Dr. Volkan was left outside. The "generous woman" was a fantasy in which he found an ideal woman who would love him unconditionally and would feed him. And his "raped girl" fantasy mirrored the superiority he felt in his relationship with the judge's daughter.

Only by the fourth year of analysis did Brown start to wonder about Dr. Volkan as a fellow human being. Recalling the Oliphant cartoons, he said, "… the tiny figures on the margin are actually even more important that the main figure. I left you outside the frame but deep down, I have always been intensely interested in you." Dr. Volkan does not talk at much length about this course of treatment, but he emphasizes that it is possible to say it was an important factor for him to understand and interpret his patient's fantasies as "transitional fantasies" (Volkan, 1973). Brown was controlling his relationship with his analyst by using his fantasies like a teddy bear (or a transitional object as described by Winnicott, 1953a, 1953b) placed between his grandiose self and Dr. Volkan.

Now, to understand Brown's narcissistic transference it will be useful to recount some things concerning Brown's progress to neurotic transference.

During the fourth year of his analysis, Brown brought up a brand-new fantasy that he called the "Henry VIII" fantasy. He was, at this time, reading a book on Henry VIII. This English king represented Brown's grandiose self. Henry VIII was enormously fat in middle age and therefore he also represented the bad mother, who was obese in Brown's early years. In his fantasy, Brown was in England as the leader of a democratic colony founded recently under a foreign power; and this was designed to bring England to democracy through Brown's good offices.

In the book he was reading, there was a footnote regarding the Turks and their power at that time—which encompassed the Siege of Vienna. Brown seemed to wish to appropriate Dr. Volkan's "power" and render it a "benign power" to be used to tame the "fat mother" through the efforts of his own grandiose self. In this fantasy, he caught and imprisoned Henry VIII, thus eliminating the influence of this cruel monarch.

Dr. Volkan summarizes the situation up to this point:

> Brown kept figuring out the meanings of his fantasies. He figured out that Henry VIII, who was overeating and therefore fat, represented his own grandiose self and his "fat" and "evil" mother along with his sense of being valueless (and hungry for love). He tried to deal with this in his relationship with the judge's daughter—and with his analyst in an act of transference. He kept them at arm's length from his grandiose self. His Henry VIII fantasy represented a "crucial juncture" experience [Klein, 1946] that integrated his images of his grandiose and his hungry self. The symbol of Henry VIII included "good" and "bad" images. He was integrating his grandiose self with his "hungry" aspect. He developed an integrated self-representation and progressed towards a neurotic personality organization.

Only after he had developed a neurotic personality organization could Brown experience the oedipal and psychosexual dimensions of his affair with the judge's daughter. The "iron ball" was not a reference to his grandiose kingdom any longer but to his testicles. While he had a narcissistic personality organization, he believed he had the best genitalia around. But now he had noticed that one of his testicles was smaller than the other. He went to a doctor who examined his testicles and told him that it was perfectly normal for a man to have testicles of differing size and that Brown was "an average (normal) man."

Dr. Volkan points out that the Brown case, with the transference he displayed in the first years of analysis, is an example of why analysts have been compelled to expand on the classical definition of this concept. Brown did not experience and feel a sense of his own hunger for love and valueless aspects; indeed, he mostly treated his analyst as if he was "nothing" without realizing that the analyst represented his own sense of worthlessness. Only in the fourth year of analysis was he able to let Dr. Volkan into his lonely but glorious kingdom. Then he owned up to the above and was able to accept being an "average man." He managed to show classical transference neurosis only after these developments.

A borderline personality organization case study

When Saul was a child, he used to sit in a corner holding himself and he appeared to live in a world of his own. He was unresponsive when addressed and by the time he was four years old, his entire vocabulary consisted of six words: hi, mom, dad, candy, pig, and goodbye. He did not start speaking properly until he was six.

Saul's rich parents were determined to get help for their son. Saul was sent to private schools and exposed to different behavioral modification techniques. So, upon reaching adolescence, Saul could speak as well as others and had started to read widely. He was sent to the famous Chestnut Lodge Hospital in his late teens where he was both an inpatient and an outpatient and he received psychoanalytically oriented individual therapy. It is possible that in this way Saul managed to evolve his inner world to the level of a borderline personality organization. After that, he was sent to Dr. Volkan for help with his developmental process. Dr. Volkan saw Saul for four sessions a week for five years.

When Saul initially came to Dr. Volkan, he had just been accepted to the University of Virginia, where Dr. Volkan worked at this time. From adolescence onwards, Saul worked mainly on mathematics, physics, astronomy, and other fields of study that have limited emotional content and require minimal social interaction. He started to believe he was a genius and was encouraged in this perception by his mother. That said, his self-representation as "retarded" continued. He also divided his object images into "genius" and "retarded." When he came to the University of Virginia, he started to live a lonely life in every aspect excepting everyday interactions involving shopping and providing for himself. He judged others on their IQ—this was his only criterion. He was overweight and walked like a penguin. He came to his sessions with greasy pants and he usually stuffed toilet paper in his pockets and underneath his shirt. Sometimes toilet paper dangled from his sleeves.

Saul told Dr. Volkan that he had been subjected to harsh potty training by his mother and that she had subjected him to numerous enemas when he had shown signs of constipation. Before long, a picture of Saul's early life began to emerge.

His Jewish father arrived in the USA from Europe as a small child and made a fortune by collecting and selling scrap metal. He was not an educated person. When he was forty, he married a Christian wife from a small town. She was a college graduate, talented in music, and twenty years his junior. Because she believed she could have been a great pianist if she had not married an older man from a different culture and religious background, she was disappointed in life. She secretly considered herself superior to her husband in terms of culture and education. In her mind, her husband was an ignorant man who had made a fortune by collecting and selling other people's filthy garbage. There was a secret "splitting" in the family. The first son belonged to the father. The mother wanted Saul, the second son, for herself, as her extension. By frequently administering enemas to the boy, she wanted him to be clean, superior, and unsullied by "filth."

Saul's first apparent indication of transference was his perception of the analyst as his mother. Toilet paper showed that he was eager to be cleaned in Dr. Volkan's practice to satisfy the highly talented and "good" analyst/ mother. However, Dr. Volkan realized in the first year of analysis that Saul could not pronounce the word "enema." Instead he would say something close to "anaemia." Dr. Volkan felt that due to her harsh ways, Saul perceived his mother as bloodsucking. His image of the "good" mother was separated from the image of the "evil" mother. In his sessions with Dr. Volkan, Saul was either a "genius" or an "idiot." For him, there was no such concept as "average."

When he first lay on the couch, Saul talked about galaxies in a most superior manner and he mocked others who did not have his compendious knowledge. Yet in some sessions he castigated himself as stupid. By the second year of analysis with Dr. Volkan, Saul therapeutically regressed by creating various fantasies of cannibalism. He had masturbation fantasies of sucking his image of his mother inside his chest and hearing her commands as internal hallucinations. Then in his psychotic transference, he mentally sucked Dr. Volkan in through his penis. At this time, he fused his internalized mother image with the analyst's image. He could not feel where his mother's image ended and where Dr. Volkan's image began. Over time, he gradually started to differentiate Dr. Volkan's image from his mother's and to separate it from his self-image.

As time passed, Saul started to be twenty-five minutes late for his appointments. Dr. Volkan generally left his office door open so his patients could walk right in, shut the door upon entering, and head for the couch. After arriving for his appointment late with a big smile on his face, Saul would lie on the couch, seemingly quite happily and tell Dr. Volkan about how things were in his life, saying, "And another thing, Dr. Volkan ..." Dr. Volkan started to be curious as to why Saul was in the habit of being twenty-five minutes late every time. He concluded that by being mentally absent for the first half of the session and present in the second, he was splitting his sessions and symbolically his self-image and his analyst's image.

Despite his curiosity, Dr. Volkan waited for about a month before probing Saul on this subject. When asked if he realized he was coming for his sessions halfway through, Saul reacted with a big smile and said, "You're completely wrong, Dr. Volkan."

Vamık Volkan:

> While he was saying that, he was in such a good mood that I too sat behind him with a smile on my face. At last, I found out that Saul would arrive on time and spent the first twenty-five minutes of his time in the bathroom next to my office. While he was there, he was imagining I was a monster, a harsh mother who performed enemas and sucked blood. My "evil" image was kept split within a bathroom that was divided from my office by one thin wall. And in my office, he was investing in me the attributes of a "good" parent and one could almost say, entertaining me.
>
> Saul was certainly splitting me and his self-representation. I hoped this to be an indicator of his starting to "split" developmentally. Further, I hoped that in the future he would be able to bring together his two opposite aspects, first with a "crucial juncture" experience. After telling me how he communicated with my image in the bathroom for twenty-five minutes prior to coming into my office, he started showing up on time for his sessions.

Saul's "crucial juncture" experience was both very tangible and dramatic. One day during a routine and rather comfortable session, Saul suddenly got off the couch and physically attacked Dr. Volkan. Although greatly taken aback by this, Dr. Volkan managed to protect himself and neither got hurt. The incident lasted several minutes, during which time Saul seemed to be

overwhelmed with emotion. It could be seen that he was also surprised—
that he had surprised himself. He left the room and Dr. Volkan thought he
was headed for the bathroom. Within a short space of time Saul returned
with a mature mien and apologized in a steady voice. He then resumed his
place on the couch. The two spent the rest of the session and some of the
next sessions analyzing this surprise attack and the consequent physical
contact with his analyst.

Vamık Volkan:

> First of all, a mistake apropos technique or an unconscious act on
> my part might have provoked this incident. But I could not identify
> it. By trying to hear Saul's association about his physical contact
> with me, I realized this incident represented the "crucial juncture"
> experience. He, as an "evil" image, contacted me, a "good" image, or
> vice versa. He felt this was the first experience of its kind for him.
> His being overwhelmed with emotion during this incident repre-
> sented his primitive need to fix opposite images. By putting our-
> selves in his place, we can imagine the panic he experienced when
> "losing" his "good" side when he had started integrating the oppo-
> sites and becoming an "average (normal) integrated individual."

Shortly after this incident, Saul started to attend meetings at The Bridge,
a Christian meeting place. It was not hard to understand that the name of
the organization attracted him. The Bridge mirrored the connection he
was constantly striving to create between his own opposite self and object
images. He was like a developing child progressing from developmental
splitting to an integrated self and also experiencing others' images as integrated. Dr. Volkan felt like a child's analyst, watching his faltering steps.

Through his association with The Bridge, Saul learned how to interact
with other people. Then he started to go to court a few days a week to attend
trials. His purpose, as he put it, was "to learn more about people." He also
stopped stuffing toilet paper under his shirt and in his pockets. He felt a
desire to sit closer to his classmates and he began to do something about
his obesity.

In sessions, Saul recounted a dream in which there was a corridor leading to four different places. A cafeteria, a barber's shop, a bookstore, and a
post office. He said the cafeteria was his mother, the barber was his father,
and he was the bookstore. He thought that Dr. Volkan was the post office

where he could obtain his mail (male) and become a man. What is interesting is that in his dream he moved his bowels in the corridor without any shame. In the dream Saul felt he had gained the freedom to defecate without the need for an enema. He was groping towards the development of a new ego function. Then, he gradually started to show interest in his analyst as a father figure. He stopped going to The Bridge and started to go to Hillel, a Jewish meeting place. The reader should remember his father was Jewish.

Some years later, Dr. Volkan came across Saul by chance:

> A long time after Saul's analysis had come to an end, I bumped into him. This was in an airport and I was running for the gate. We looked at each other in some surprise. He told me he had become a psychologist and he lectured in a university.

The Saul case is a good example of when defensive splitting turns into developmental splitting after awakening in transference. The transference story here reflects the need for the development of new ego functions (integrative functions) for the development of a broken self.

A psychotic personality organization case study

Ricky was eighteen when Dr. Volkan saw him for the first time. Another psychiatrist had referred him along with the following information.

Ricky was born with a deformed right hand and right foot, with the fingers and toes of his right hand and foot longer than his fingers and toes of the left hand and foot. From his fourth birthday on, his mother gave him "wedding rings" as birthday presents. These rings were large and they did not fit his deformed fingers. His mother never openly talked to Ricky about his deformities. The psychiatrist he was initially sent to was aware that his mother was quite incompetent in teaching Ricky about reality. When Ricky was in high school, a girl told him his voice sounded different. He interpreted what the girl said as her intimating that his penis was as deformed as his hands. Before long, he became psychotic. He read every book he could find on Nazi Germany. His ideal was not to be like Adolf Hitler, but rather to be like Joseph Goebbels, Hitler's right-hand man. Goebbels had a deformed leg. Ricky thought he could spook others by portraying his mother as Hitler and himself as Goebbels. The first psychiatrist told Dr. Volkan that by acting in this way Ricky was struggling to cope with castration anxiety.

The psychiatrist added that Ricky was as obedient to his cruel mother as Goebbels was to Hitler. When Ricky reached the age of sixteen, his mother, as usual, gave him a golden wedding ring as a birthday present and the next day his parents committed him to a mental institution. He was duly placed in a ward with other mentally disturbed young people and was put on medication. A psychiatrist talked to Ricky at odd moments and told him he was not actually castrated. As time went by there was an improvement in Ricky's psychological state. He was no longer talking about Hitler and Goebbels. Still, the psychiatrist noticed he was constantly walking with an unnaturally stiff gait reminiscent of Nazi soldiers. The psychiatrist thought this was his way of rejecting castration. Ricky was making his body an erect penis. When Ricky was released, Dr. Volkan was asked to treat him as an outpatient. Dr. Volkan was briefed by the hospital psychiatrist, and relates:

> Listening to the doctor, I realized I was hearing another strange story about how a mother used her child probably to counter the narcissistic damage, anger, and guilt she felt at giving birth to a child with a physical deformity. I realized Ricky had more problems than a castration anxiety. Ricky did not have a neurotic personality organization and oedipal conflict. His obsession with the Nazis and his identifying his mother with Hitler and himself as Goebbels reflected aggressive pre-oedipal experiences that fragmented his self and object images. By the way, I should state that Ricky's family is not Jewish. The obsession therefore cannot come from that. It is rather that, for Ricky, Hitler, Goebbels, and the Nazis in general became global symbols of extreme aggression.

In the first two sessions Dr. Volkan observed how Ricky held his body upright and rigid. He was walking like a Nazi soldier marching past Hitler.

Ricky was interested in the objects in Dr. Volkan's office, such as the paintings on the walls and the books. Dr. Volkan felt that he was familiarizing himself with his new environment. In the middle of his third session Ricky suddenly stopped talking and started to make sucking noises as his eyelids got heavier.

Vamık Volkan:

> There was a sign with my name on it in the corridor. Three other doctors' doors opened onto the same corridor and they also had

their names on the wall. Ricky told me that before he entered my room for the third session he read my name Vamık Volkan again. He reached the conclusion that I was a German "as strong as Hitler." He had previously noticed my accent and felt that I was not of American origin. He informed me that he imagined drinking German wine and spitting it out. If he had been a person with neurotic personality organization, I would probably have waited to hear the patient's opinions about me without saying anything. It was important to create a "reality base" for Ricky. I told him I was not German but ethnically Turkish. Without hesitation, he asked me, "Do the Turks make wine too?" And I answered, "Yes." He then asked me, "Do the Turks make sweet or sour wine?" Knowing that he would perceive both as a "good" and "bad" object, "Both," I answered. I asked him to choose one. Ricky chose me as sweet wine and made a gesture with his mouth indicating me in an exaggerated manner and then seemed to relax.

In his third session Ricky let it be known that he had an inner voice with a Turkish accent telling him what to do. This represented his keeping Dr. Volkan's image as a "good" Turk inside his self. Yet, at the same time he had another inner voice with a German accent telling him not to heed the first inner voice—interactions among his fragmented internalized images. This went on for many months.

Vamık Volkan:

When my internalized object image competed with his "Hitler mother" image, Ricky usually became perplexed. I told him there was no hurry in choosing between the two voices. After all, the Turkish accent was pretty new to him. I also told him he was still not sure whether this voice with a Turkish accent would help him or not. He shouldn't rush into anything.

In the second year of treatment, Dr. Volkan discovered that Ricky was reading history books about Turks instead of books on Nazi Germany. He became confused when he read about Turks being "warmongers." He was unable to differentiate between Turks and Nazis. Dr. Volkan's image also became a "bad" one. In sessions, Ricky started to whistle in order to blank Dr. Volkan's image out (to prevent its internalization and introjection through his ears). Dr. Volkan put up with this for some time; he also told Ricky that he could tell him at any time whether he perceived his analyst as frightening, that his analyst had no intention of killing him, and that, at the same time, he was unable to make Ricky's fingers and toes more shapely. Dr. Volkan tried to fashion the image of a man telling his son the realities.

After this the whistling stopped. Dr. Volkan realized that Ricky was using him as a love object. He had started to dream of eating Turkish delight.

> 'Did I know the exact distance between Charlottesville and Washington?' I asked him to find the answers himself in order to develop autonomy. When he resisted, I told him I would just wait until he found out the distance between Charlottesville and Washington. This would enhance a relationship between two informed people. This can be most pleasurable.

As time passed Ricky began to sexualize his eating Turkish delight. This behavior mirrored the gradual development of his father transference and he began experiencing Dr. Volkan as an oedipal father as a neurotic patient would. He ceased to be preoccupied by the Nazis. And his analysis ended a couple of months after he started dating a young woman for the first time in his life.

CHAPTER EIGHT

Various aspects of large-group psychology

With Jimmy Carter in Atlanta, Georgia in 1992.

With the former Cyprus president Glafcos Klerides, Atlanta, Georgia, 1992.

Welcoming Mikhail Gorbachev and Raisa Gorbacheva to Charlottesville, Virginia, 1993.

With the Turkish President Abdullah Gül in Ankara, 2008.

The term "large group" in psychoanalytic literature usually signifies groups of at least 30 to 150 at most, coming together to handle a particular problem. As for Dr. Volkan, he uses the term "large group" to define tens of thousands or millions of people (as in "we are Apache, we are Lithuanian Jews, we are Ukrainian, we are Kurdish, we are Polish, we are Cypriot Turks, we are white, we are Muslim, we are communists") who are interconnected with a persistent sameness perception and the sharing of collective subjective experiences, whether they be those of a tribe, a clan, a class, or ethnicity, race, nationality, religion, or political ideology.

Most of the individuals in such large groups never encounter one another throughout their lives. Indeed, they are not even aware of the existence of most of the people with whom they share the large-group identity. Members of a large group share some values we can call "cultural amplifiers" (Mack, 1979) such as common bodily features, language, nursery rhymes, food, dances, religion or other mystical beliefs, mythology, the flag, and most importantly, as Vamık Volkan concluded while concerned with international affairs, the images held by group members of real or mythological figures or places or historical events. The cultural amplifiers of a large group are only related to that group. The people of a given group have a shared narcissistic investment in it and this is a source of pride and a sign of "superiority." If they dwell on the collective pain stemming from a historical event they have experienced, this may be seen as "much greater" than the pain of others.

Individual identity

Sigmund Freud seldom referred to the term "identity." Yet one well-known reference to identity is found in a speech Freud delivered to the Jewish organization B'nai B'rith in 1926. He was not actually the speaker due to his debilitation as cancer set in and another read the text he had prepared. Freud wondered why he was bound to Jewry since, as a non-believer, he had never been instilled with ethno-national pride or religious faith. Nevertheless, Freud noted a "safe privacy of a common mental construction," and a clear consciousness of his "inner identity" (as a Jew) (1941e, p. 274). It is interesting that Freud's remarks linked his individual identity with his large-group identity.

In Dr. Volkan's opinion, for many years, psychoanalysts addressed the issue of large-group identity without using the word identity. This may seem strange—because it is. They also looked at the issue without studying either

Vamık Volkan with Erik Erikson and Joan Erikson, Big Sur, California, 1982.

flashpoints or peacemaking among peoples. It was Erik Erikson who turned "identity" into a psychoanalytic concept. He first used the expression "ego identity," then dropped the word ego. He defined identity as "a persistent sameness within oneself ... [and] a persistent sharing of essential characteristics with others" (1956, p. 57).

In psychoanalysis there is a consensus that the identity of an individual expresses a subjective experience. According to Dr. Volkan, identity differs from similar, perhaps interchangeable, concepts such as "character" or "personality." The concepts of character and personality reflect others' impressions about people's emotional expressions, the way they speak, their idiosyncrasies, their attitudes.

Having completed his first psychiatry education at the University of Virginia with Dr. Volkan after he came to the USA from India, Salman Akhtar, now a psychoanalyst known worldwide, looked at an indivdiual's identity from different perspectives. According to Akhtar (1984), a temporal persistency accompanies the internal sameness feeling in the experience of identity. The past, present, and future coalesce in the array of the individual's recollections, and felt and expected existence. Individual identity is connected to a realistic body image and a feeling of internal integrity, and it is related to the capacity for being alone and the openness of his or her gender. Akhtar also associates individual identity with large-group identity such as national, ethnic, or religious identities. The last characteristic of individual identity that Akhtar cites is the connection between individual identity and large-group identity—one that he asserts will develop during the oedipal phase. He suggests that complete integration of children with the large-group identity within themselves occurs around the age of four or five. At these ages, children identify with their parents' ideals and limits and thereupon their large group's ideals and limits.

As I stated earlier, according to research carried out on newborns in recent years, a newborn's mind works much more actively than had been thought at the time that Dr. Volkan embarked on his higher education. For instance, in a study Robert Emde conducted on the evolution of the newborn mind it is suggested that there are group-related behaviors and a psychobiological potential towards the perception of "we-ness" (Emde, 1991). In a book by Paul Bloom (2010), psychology professor at Yale, it is persuasively argued that what and why we love what we do from early childhood onwards is a key factor in our unfolding inclination towards our own large group. Bloom mentions that a three-month-old baby pays more attention to the face of someone from the same race and that children like dressing in the same colors and in the same style as adults within their own group.

Because the social sphere of a newborn or a little child is limited to the parents, brothers and sisters, relatives, and other caregivers, it does not include different dimensions of "we-ness" in terms of large-group identity. A newborn child is in an "all inclusive attitude when group tendencies, nationality, ethnicity, religion, and political ideology are considered" (Erikson, 1985). Subjective experience with respect to belonging to a large group develops later.

Large-group identity

Large-group identity is an abstract concept formed by hundreds of thousands or millions of people sharing a language, religion, cuisine, dances, cultural symbols, traditions, enemies, mythologized images of historical events, or sense of ethnicity. Sometimes togetherness arises from a shared political ideology, such as communism or Nazism, particularly if children grow up under such ideologies. From childhood, people feel they are the same as their fellow members of the large group even if they will never see them in their lives.

Everyone has a genetic identity. This, needless to say, is present from birth. Yet the individual identity or large-group identity of a child is not there when a child is born. The very young child is neutral; she (or he— either can apply throughout this chapter) does not feel that she belongs to a large group. The child drinks milk, eats, and sleeps and, we hope, develops physically. In parallel with this, if we are to metaphorically express the relationships the child establishes with her parents, siblings, relatives, neighbors, or friends, she "eats" enough to develop a psychological identity. How we internalize our relationships, emotions, traumas, and love constitutes the foundation of our personal identity. A child born into a Greek family in Istanbul is baptized in the Greek Orthodox manner with the Greek language as the idiom. Before this child begins to comprehend the world around him, his family feeds him some kinds of food that would never be given to a Turkish child born in Istanbul. Being initially neutral and without a feeling of belonging to any particular group, the child will then, willingly or not, abandon this neutrality.

By identifying first with their parents and relatives and then with their teachers and other important people around them, children unknowingly fuse the core of their personal identity with a large-group identity. The child differentiates the language, traditions, and symbols of her own large group from other large groups.

When the child stops being, in Erik Erikson's (1985) term, a "generalist" in relation to tribal tendencies, nationality, ethnicity, and religious or political ideologies, subjective experiences related to belonging to a large group start to develop.

Vamık Volkan:

> Existing environmental conditions lead children to invest in large-group identities. For instance, a child born in Hyderabad will focus on religious/cultural matters in the course of developing a large-group identity because the adults around him see their dominant large-group identities as Muslim or Hindu according to their families' religious orientations. Similarly, a child born in Cyprus in a period when relations between Cypriot Turks and Cypriot Greeks are tense will absorb a dominant large-group identity defined by ethnic/national/political feelings. In troubled times, being a Cypriot Greek or a Cypriot Turk assumes a critical importance over and above being an Orthodox Christian or a Sunni Muslim. In terms of large-group identity, the matter of investing oneself in ethnicity or religion, in nationality or race, is something that happens without any particular ideology or belief system being that important. What is necessary to understand is the psychodynamic process that links individual identity to large-group identity and how large groups use these links in their interactions.

In the course of adolescence, an individual experiences a psychological review within. The adolescent starts to modify the investments important people made in her images in her childhood and transforms the identifications she made with them; she strengthens some and others, she ignores. Furthermore, beyond the limited environment composed of family and other relatives, she now starts to establish new identifications with the experiences she has with her peer groups. Through these internal activities, the youngster's internal sense of sameness is thus reviewed (Blos, 1979). Formation of a solid identity is completed at this stage with children's perceptions of large-group identity and of how belonging to a particular large group differentiates them from other large-group identities. By adolescence, according to Dr. Volkan, membership of a large group is cemented for life. For those who have emigrated, willingly or not, and for those who for intellectual or other reasons reject membership, the membership is still there in a shadowy way.

When an international conflict arises between different large groups, children tend to have psychological problems which can stretch into adulthood. While Dr. Volkan was working in South Ossetia from 1998 to 2002 he observed how the conflict between the South Ossetians and the Georgians created considerable disturbance in the minds of those whose origins and ties were on both sides of the divide. He noted the same trouble with children born of Hungarian–Romanian marriages.

Winnicott's circle

In 1969, Donald Winnicott drew a diagram of a man by a circle. He explained that the inner part of the circle is full of forces structuring the internal reality of a person. He added:

> An individual mature enough to be represented by a circle is capable of covering the conflicts arising from within or without; and this circle needs to be split with a line drawn down the middle because along the line in the middle there always has to be a conflict, or a potential conflict. Groups composing of benign and malignant factors are present on both sides of the line. (pp. 222–223)

Winnicott writes that only idealistic people talk about people who have nothing within them but good forces utilized for good purposes—like a circle without a line through the middle.

Winnicott holds that the individual is a relatively modern concept. He says that until a few centuries ago, everyone was in a non-integrated state except for a few extraordinary "integrated individuals." According to Dr. Volkan, Winnicott thought even at the time of writing that the world was generally composed of people who could not accomplish the integration stage and could not, therefore, be whole.

Yet, Vamık Volkan thinks it would be less confusing to think that a circle with a line in the middle represents an individual who can tolerate ambivalent feelings to a degree. If the subject is approached in metapsychological terms, an individual whose opposite halves touch each other in the circle has a personality organization higher than the previous level—the personality organization level—compared to an individual whose halves do not touch.

In a diagram representing someone who cannot achieve true integration, there will be no line in the middle; instead, there will be a gap between the opposite halves of the circle. What Saul (from the previous chapter) revealed was the situation of a person who is not completely integrated, one who has the "normal" inner world of a small child who has not yet reached integration.

Before the stage where the circle is divided in two, as it were, a person can expel one of the opposite objects (i.e., one image) from his mind in order to lessen the tension arising between the non-integrated "bad" and "good" objects. Another way is to project one of these non-integrated parts onto other people or objects through a process called "externalization." Dr. Volkan suggests this example. A child who trips and falls down and gets upset about it might say it was not him who fell but his teddy bear—who did not know how to run. A child who watches someone eat ice cream with great pleasure can pretend it is he who is actually eating the ice cream. These bad or good parts do not usually stay in the places where they are externalized, but rather come back in a process called "internalization." Externalization and internalization are sequential processes.

Earlier in this book we observed such processes of externalization and internalization in adults who have not been through a successful integration process in childhood. Ricky's story (from the previous chapter) exemplifies this. Now we can examine such processes when they are shared by a group of individuals.

Externalization and internalization in large groups

As we have learned, Cypriot Turks and Greeks lived side by side for centuries until 1974 when the island was de facto divided into two separate political structures. Greek farmers often raised pigs. Turkish children were as interested in farm animals as Greek children were, as indeed most children are wherever they come from. Imagine a Turkish child wanting to touch or pet a piglet. His mother or other Turkish adults important to the child will most likely be horrified by this, as for Muslims the pig is an unclean animal. The Turkish child perceives the pig as a cultural amplifier for the Greeks. Pigs are not part of the large-group identity of the Turkish people. This way, the Turkish child finds a reservoir to permanently externalize his non-integrated "bad" self—and object images. Since Turkish Muslims do not generally eat pork or raise pigs, the externalized image of the pig will not be perceptibly reinternalized (Volkan, 1988).

When the child finds a suitable target for his bad self and object images, the idea of the "other" begins to take shape at an experimental level in the child's mind. At this stage, a Turkish child cannot exactly comprehend what "Greekness" means. Images about the "other," subtle thoughts, perceptions, and feelings will develop much later, before the individual realizes that the first symbol of the "enemy" has helped rid him of the tension arising from his object relations. Because almost all the Turkish children in Cyprus will use the same images, they will share the same premises regarding the "other"—who can then be turned into the "enemy" as problems in the real world crowd in.

Vamık Volkan cites Norman Itzkowitz telling him of some children of Polish Jewish origin living in the USA, far from the deadly danger of the anti-Semitic Old World. They were taught to spit three times on passing a Catholic church. This behavior could be dismissed as mere superstition, but according to Itzkowitz, it was also a result of the church being used as a suitable externalization object. Dr. Volkan endorses this view and adds, "In relatively safe environments, it is certainly easier to ditch the 'bad' externalization objects, but memories are long." Alongside Poles, of course, all manner of people have flocked to the USA in search of the American identity, to buy into an idealized version of this large group. For this reason, their patterns of externalization are more complex and changeable than those of Cypriot Turks living in Cyprus.

In 1984, Dr. Volkan assumed the leadership of the team convoked by the American Psychiatric Association to bring together prominent Israeli, Palestinian, and Egyptian delegates. He noted of a meeting held in Switzerland in that year:

> In that meeting I fully understood the crucial factor of large-group identity in international relations.
>
> On the first day of this meeting, I was sitting in a little group on the left-hand side of General Shlomo Gazit, a well-known retired soldier, who was sitting next to a Palestinian psychiatrist from Gaza. Suddenly, the Palestinian turned to the Israeli general and said: "You are the first and last Israeli general who was fair in the affairs with the Arabs. I don't like living under Israeli blockade, not one little bit. But as a human being, I respect you. After your tour ended, none of the other Israeli commanders treated us anywhere near as fairly as you did."

> The Palestinian seemed rather agitated as he talked. He put his right hand in his trouser pocket. I could see the anxious movement of his finger beneath the fabric. At that moment, I wondered if sitting beside an Israeli general who had enforced the blockade of Gaza had triggered in him a castration anxiety and that he was touching his penis as reassurance that it was still there. He was almost screaming, "As long as I have this, you can't take my Palestinian identity away from me." Well, he couldn't have meant his member and I tried to speculate as to what object he had in his pocket that was so vital to him.

Sometime later Dr. Volkan found his answer. The Palestinian psychiatrist had been holding on to a small stone he carried dyed in the colors of the Palestinian flag. He did not show this stone to Dr. Volkan, only described it. He also gave Dr. Volkan to understand that many of his compatriots carried similar stones and that they held great meaning, indeed they endowed a sense of security and a feeling of solidarity. In difficult times, and times are always difficult for the Palestinians, the little colored stones act as a symbol of the externalized ethnic identity of their people. And these symbolic objects are hidden from Israeli eyes.

Nations

Vamık Volkan believes that literature, history, political science, sociology, anthropology, and philosophy are a fruitful source of phenomenology defining tribal, ethnic, national, and religious groups. He adds that the definition of a large group often varies depending on the discipline of the person defining it. The word "nation" is used to define a large group of people who have a mutual living space, a shared past, language, lifestyle, and economy. However, another definition of the word nation could be the people living in a particular region affiliated to the same state, a community of people living within the legal boundaries of a state. Others suggest the word "nation" should not be associated with "state." A simple definition of a large group is not enough to explain policies, economics, laws, and the power to influence military matters.

Superficial definitions are also far from explaining strategies adopted by large groups to inhibit the possibility of peaceful coexistence with others. Add to that the shifts in perceived identity that will inevitably occur in polities of thousands or millions in the light of historical events such as revolutions, changing economic conditions, invasions, migrations, the personalities of political leaders, and so on. In this regard, Dr. Volkan presents Turkey as an example:

> As we have said, shortly after the founding of the Turkish Republic in 1923, the fez, which was a type of hat worn by men as a cultural amplifier, was out. It was seen by the modernizers in charge as incompatible with the process of modernization and Westernization. But in the Turkey of today, religious identity symbols have come to overshadow national symbols. This is a very significant shift that needs examining. It seems to me to be more useful to study psychodynamic processes at play in relationships within the large group or with other large groups rather than getting tied up in superficial definitions of what constitutes a polity.

Synthetic nations

Nation states have been born in different ways. Sometimes diverse people voluntarily coalesce into a state such as the USA. Of course, African slaves were not consenting participants in this. Israel is another example, although again there are the non-consenting among the population in the shape of Arabs, many of whom do not wish to live under Israeli rule. The USA and Israel we can call "synthetic nations" (Loewenberg, 1994, 1995). As the psychoanalyst and historian Peter Loewenberg argues, such nations require a common mythologized past, usually vainglorious and sometimes packed with harrowing stories of its own suffering, generally characterized by self-love, in order to strengthen the synthesis.

The attempt to establish a bond between the diverse often involves projecting negative attributes onto other peoples so that one's own large group will be thrown into positive relief. In the USA, the "white" majority used (to a lesser extent still use) an idealized white identity to characterize the synthesis of the nation. Of course, this involves racism. In Dr. Volkan's opinion, the Jewish children's ritual of detestation of the Catholic Church discussed above pales into insignificance before the main externalized target of white Americans—those with the "wrong" skin pigmentation. Even now, after an African American has served two terms as their elected president, the USA still has a long way to go in terms of combating racism.

In 2001, Vamık Volkan was invited to celebrate the fifty-second anniversary of the foundation of the Israeli state. At the venue of Mount Herzl, the national memorial to the west of Jerusalem, on May 10, Avraham Burg, speaker of the Knesset, gave the keynote speech. A short while before, Volkan and Burg had a meeting in the Knesset on the subject of cultural differences and peaceful coexistence. Burg had contended that no nation had ever overcome such a trauma as the Holocaust, or paid such a high price on the battlefield in establishing a state as Israel had. Yet he also expressed dissatisfaction at the way Israel had turned out. He felt that people were eager to get under their own particular tent. To Dr. Volkan, Burg's desire for an integrated Israel was obvious. But he was also aware this was not easy to achieve.

In his speech at Mount Herzl Burg said:

> Israel is a community composed of beliefs and people who have various beliefs. There is only one God and four religions: Judaism, Christianity, Islam and Druze. Religious and secular people, Jews and Arabs, men and women, the rich and the poor, Westerners and Easterners, immigrants and those born in Israel …

He was clearly aware of the identity problem in Israel. "We have to carry the identity dispute from here, from Mount Herzl to daily life, to classrooms, workplaces, parliament and other decision-making bodies." After Burg's speech, representatives of twelve different groups directly affected by genocide and persecution such as European Israelis, African Jews, and immigrants from Russia mounted the podium to express their solidarity.

The Palestinian large-group identity was also forged in trauma, loss of life, and utter humiliation. The Palestinian identity has developed with a sense of being the most put upon of all the Arabs and it could be said to exist under a flag of suffering. The sense of suffering is often used in the formation of a sense of moral superiority and the latent or open expression of masochistic large-group narcissism (Volkan & Fowler, 2009).

> Returning to my observations from the year 2001, it could be said that there is a psychological need to have enemies while creating a "synthetic" nation. Having said this, we can account for the question

of why it is still so hard to find a peaceful solution to the Israel–Palestine problem. This does not entail underestimating the actual problems. Understanding the basic underlying psychological factors in an international conflict does not clear away the problems, but it can be a guide for the resolution of conflicts.

Enemies

In his book *The Need to Have Enemies and Allies*, Vamık Volkan (1988) explains how the concept of the "enemy" develops in childhood. Those belonging to "other" large groups might potentially become our enemies in the future. We develop a bias against the other. This is a natural psychological phenomenon. Everyone has biases. We call this "normal" or "innocuous" bias. If the bias becomes dangerous for some reason, personal and social problems emerge. Dr. Volkan looks at this from a Cypriot perspective:

> The EOKA member who shot Erol became a killer to increase the narcissism and power of his large group, to hurt the large-group identity of the Cypriot Turks, and because of his dangerous biases. We may speculate that this unknown assailant felt no remorse for what he did due to these biases. This was one man. Multiply that by hundreds of thousands or indeed millions and such things can lead to catastrophe. I wouldn't want you to think that I am speaking out against Cypriot Greeks, that I am castigating them with the bogey of EOKA. Far from it. Having spent decades in areas of conflict in many parts of the world, I find that there are similar psychological processes in each large group. For various historical reasons, sometimes this large group or that large group has used these common psychological processes, for instance dangerous biases, to hurt or destroy the "demonized other." This unfortunate phenomenon has plagued millennia.
>
> We all saw this close up thanks to instant media coverage during the collapse of Yugoslavia towards the end of the last century. In this instance, Serbian leader Slobodan Milosević, bent on carving out a Greater Serbia, mobilized his people's large-group identity with horrific consequences (see Volkan, 1996, 2004).

The "Who are we?" inquiry

Identities are always sought out. We can imagine that back in the mists of time a group wore red feathers on their heads and developed a bias towards those who wore green feathers. And so, a clash. We can also be fairly sure that primitive societies fought over food and women. As the human mind developed, more sophisticated concepts, such as prestige, ethnicity, religious opinions, and political ideologies began to take their place in large-group conflicts. Throughout history there have been events changing and adding new features to large-group identity. Wars of independence tend to be fought to achieve a "separate identity."

There are trends. For example, the emerging nations of Europe in a new ideological age turned to revolution and the imposition of their leaders' ideas on what kind of large-group identity they should have. In the case of the French revolutionaries, this involved decapitating the king and queen and a great many besides. Having disposed of the ancient regime, the revolutionaries took it upon themselves to dictate what the national identity should be. Indeed, they decided that the very calendar should be changed to reflect the revolution and year one was no longer the estimated date of Christ's birth, but the date of their elevation to power (Davies, 1996). Yet the large-group concept of democracy that we espouse today began to arise in its modern form at this time.

With the demise of the European overseas empires and the collapse of the Soviet Empire, we have seen great changes in the way various peoples see themselves. A preoccupation with "ethnicity" has arisen and the various ethnic groups have blurred themselves to a large extent in their geographical manifestations through mass migration. The "shrinkage and stirring of the world" caused by advanced forms of communication involves a vast amount of incoming information about other peoples and their mores. This begs the question, "Who are we now?"

Vamık Volkan's works explore the issues raised by this question, particularly those connected to seeking out identity.

As Norman Itzkowitz puts it, the world has entered an "ethnic" phase. As we know, this trend has spread to Turkey. When opinions and feelings about common religious identity are mixed with the "Who are we now?" question, complications arise and there can be regressions in societies. Globalization and instant communication facilitated by very advanced technology has been our shared experience for the last few decades. Globalization is a phenomenon which encapsulates certain ideals. It is supposed to benefit all large groups in the world—when everything goes right. Yet, in reality, the phenomenon of the interests of multinationals rolling over those of others, exploitation of cheap labor, child labor, and seemingly ineradicable racism have soured the idealized image of globalization. We are seeing new assessments of the impact of globalization and perhaps we are also seeing gropings towards new forms of civilization.

Time collapse

The title of this section deals with clothes. Clearly, when people put on certain clothes, they put on identity. A school uniform can foster team spirit. A military uniform even more so. A man donning a tuxedo might feel that thereby his identity has a great deal to do with having a high social status. One could go on indefinitely. Vamık Volkan has extrapolated from his work in the field of large groups that clothing can cause a kind of "time collapse" with certain forms of garb being redolent with the history and culture for the wearer. Would it be too much to say that clothes can change an ordinary person into a suicide bomber?

Vamık Volkan:

> Now, let's imagine we have had two forms of dress since childhood. The first is the type which clothes the body and forms an expression of our personal identity. The second is what we might call a collective form of dress. Perhaps we can use the metaphor of a very big canvas tent under which thousands or millions gather. At "normal" times, we pay attention to clothing the body. In our everyday life, we are occupied with matters such as our family, relatives, friends, our job, career, our sports club, how we make money, where we go for our holidays, what's happened on Facebook. When times are less tranquil the large group's clothing assumes great importance. If those living under another tent knowingly and willfully throw mud at or try to damage the large-group canvas under which we live, then we struggle to clean, repair, and protect the canvas. When millions are engaged in this shared struggle, it can become a social and political situation from which terrorism can emerge.

To develop our metaphor, let us see the canvas under which a large group lives decorated with symbols which are unique to them, impressed like a seal on each part. These symbols reflect events from the distant and mythologized past. Very often political leaders have resuscitated these images for their own purposes. For instance, the Serbian propaganda machine at the time of Slobodan Milosević reactivated the image of the Battle of Kosovo fought 600 years before. Events like this bring a situation to light in what I call a "time collapse." The feelings, perceptions, and thoughts about a long bygone historical event are rekindled in the minds of the many and they merge with their feelings, perceptions, and thoughts about today's "enemy." The perceived threat and the perceived wickedness of today's enemy are greatly augmented in this way. Bosnian people were killed because they were perceived to be Ottomans. This, we contend, was a product of what we describe above.

When the pictures sealed on the canvas are covered in mud thrown by the enemy and when homes are wrecked by the "other," those under the canvas feel frightened and humiliated and consequently cling to their large-group identity all the more. Together they strive to repair the tent along with all its decor, all its symbols.

Erol's killer or people who take to the mountains to become terrorists and suicide bombers may all have personal reasons for their actions. Still, if we examine such people close up, that is, when we are able to, we can see that they are not under the influence of their personal psychology but under the influence of their large-group identity psychology. Those in charge of training suicide bombers in Palestine some years ago put the young people destined for this fate through one or two years of training, part of which was to clothe them in the large-group canvas in lieu of their personal clothing. Young people whose parents had been humiliated or killed by the "enemy," or whose own identities had been hurt, were groomed to become violent representatives of their large group. As time passed and the canvas of the Palestinians and other Arabs became more frayed and ravaged, the period of training became shorter *ad absurdum*. A suicide bomber could be prepared within twenty-four hours. As the attack on the large-group identity grew, many people living under the tent could volunteer to protect it even if they had not been personally injured. And the individual's actual clothing is very much part of the identity being asserted and being seen as under attack.

"Pseudo species" and killing in the name of large-group identity

In November 2006, Dr. Volkan received an invitation to make the opening speech of the celebration of Archbishop Desmond Tutu's seventy-fifth birthday and the tenth anniversary of the Truth and Reconciliation Commission at the University of Cape Town in South Africa. He made his speech and then spent some time at the Kruger National Park, a place of extraordinary beauty with a myriad of protected wildlife and with various secure hides reflecting the dangerous nature of some of the animals. On a four-hour safari Vamık Volkan hoped to get lucky and see something spectacular.

> I am not an expert on animal behavior, but things come into my mind as I watch them. I witnessed an "oedipal story" displayed by the elephants we observed from our vehicle. There was a strange smell in the air which our guide told us came from a bull elephant who was sexually stimulated—testosterone. This elephant saw another bull elephant, which was older than him, beside two females and calves. The young bull barged in on this family gathering and caused the female elephants to run away with their babies. The two males started to fight. We watched them for a while but then we had to go. We saw other interesting spectacles. Some rhinos were spooked by thunder and started more or less dancing around a water hole in what could be termed a ritual of "we-ness." We also observed a female lion whose offspring had been killed a few days before showing affection to the offspring of another lioness. And we saw a wooden cross under a tree, marking the spot where a safari guide had gone to relieve himself and had been eaten by a lion.
>
> At the end of the day, while I was sitting somewhere safe contemplating the events of the day, I decided to jot down my observations on what the animals were doing that day in Kruger Park. They were struggling to find food, demarking their territory, expressing sexual desire and the wish to reproduce, protecting their offspring, losing their loved ones, forming a group, competing with the other males in the same group, exhibiting aggression and submission, experiencing

With Desmond Tutu, in Atlanta, Georgia, 1994.

fear, defending others of the same species, retreating [from] or fight-ing and killing the "other," and trying to survive individually and as a group. I was told that the two bull elephants which had come to blows had no intention of killing each other. The creatures who got killed in Kruger Park were dispatched by animals of a different spe-cies as in the case of the hapless tour guide taking his last leak and the elegant impalas roaming in large herds.

Clearly, most animals do not seek to kill members of their own species, although some chimpanzees engage in intraspecies violence that looks simi-lar to humans at war (Goodall, 2010). As the psychologist Norman Dixon puts it, "… man is the only species which through his ability to kill at a distance cannot avail himself of those automatic inhibitors of intra-species aggres-sion which are commonplace with other animals" (1976, p. 66). Why people should be able to slaughter each other, often without hesitation, in the name of their large-group identity seems an important field of research.

One explanation for this horrific conundrum could be what Dr. Volkan calls the phenomenon of the "pseudo species." The term was coined by Erik Erikson (1985) to signify the differences that humans perceive and designate among themselves. Erikson says that man has evolved since the dawn of time as if there were different species of humans marked out from each other by some supernatural intervention. Hence, we have clans, tribes, and social classes. Erikson puts forward the hypothesis that primitive man put on clothing torn from animals and that tribal identity became linked to the resulting "look." Dr. Volkan concurs with Erikson and believes that humans can kill one another so readily because they have the notion that they are a different species and their garb is used to accentuate this perceived difference.

Vamık Volkan comes to the conclusion that this assumption of Erikson's is speculative and he can add another notion as to what happened in the evolutionary process of mankind. For centuries, neighboring tribes have interacted with each other across natural boundaries. Neighboring groups have had to compete with one another for land, food, sex, and so on. As they have evolved, more psychological factors have emerged as an admixture to this competition: prestige, honor, power, envy, vengeance, humiliation, submission, and loss have all come into play. Also at play are historical memories pregnant with narcissism, identity issues, and the self-esteem of a large group shored up by religion, group symbols, traditions, and a sense of where one is in the historical continuum.

Erikson's contentions are supported by references to historical incidences of labeling the "other." Dr. Volkan notes that the ancient Chinese called themselves human and others *kuei*, or "hunting spirits." The Apaches held themselves to be *indeh*, meaning human being and others *indiah*, enemy (Boyer, 1986). The Munduruku of the Brazilian rainforests divide the world into two as Munduruku, men, and non-Munduruku, *pariwats* (enemies), with generous exceptions for some of their neighbors (Murphy, 1957). Howard Stein, an anthropologist, says this pattern "cannot be generalized for all cultures; but in feelings towards 'non-humans,' in extreme cases there can be adumbrated a universal tendency in the way peoples perceive each other and behave towards each other when they have dehumanized their fellow beings" (1990, p. 118). In historical times there are many examples of this phenomenon, but a few instances will have to suffice. The treatment meted out by Christian Europeans towards Jews in the Middle Ages and by white Americans towards African Americans in the USA, the acts of the Nazis, the atrocities carried out in the former Yugoslavia and in Rwanda, and the violence which is ongoing in Gaza are all examples of large groups dehumanizing each other.

When polities break up on (perceived) ethnic lines and erstwhile friends turn against each other, the conflict can be more bitter and protracted than conventional wars. It is not hard to see why this is so. If an unknown person thousands of miles away insults you, so what? If your friend of many years' standing insults you, it matters. Far much more so if they actually attack you. When they do, the question of identity arises, as it most certainly has done in Cyprus. The questions might be: "Are we Turkish Cypriots or Cypriot Turks?" "Is there a group identity difference between the Turkish mainlanders settling in Cyprus following the events of 1974 and the Turkish-speaking people whose families have lived on the island for centuries?" "What is the nature of the disagreement between those who think Cypriot Turks and Cypriot Greeks can live together as brothers and sisters and those who believe such a notion to be moonshine?" "What is your take on these issues as you read these lines?" As we have examined, the big question is, "Who are we?" It is a rather troubling question, particularly as it arises both from the past and the future.

CHAPTER NINE

A case study of a large group under stress: the birds of Cyprus

Greek and Turkish participants of an unofficial diplomatic meeting, Caux, Switzerland, 2000.

The eleven-year history of the Turkish Cypriot enclaves can be divided into two periods, during the first of which (1963–1968) Turks were actually imprisoned within them. During the second, between 1968 and the Turkish military coming to the island in 1974, they were "free" to move out of them and to pass through Greek Cypriot territory to visit, but the land they had fled in 1963–1964 was not available to them for resettlement.

In the summer of 1968, Dr. Volkan returned to Cyprus after a prolonged absence. He noticed that the houses he frequented in the Nicosia enclave, and the one which belonged to his parents and in which he stayed, had a great many caged birds, always parakeets, and he watched the feeding of these creatures with great interest. Vamık's family proudly showed him the birds—the "daughter-in-law" moving into her new house (the cage), the "mother and father," and a barren but energetic female parakeet that was their special pet. So ubiquitous were the caged birds among the Cypriot Turks that Vamık found them in public buildings, coffee shops, and stores. He recalls having to jump over birdcages to get into a grocers. Sometimes the cages were homemade and several generations of birds were packed into the same space. The locals set great store by these birds and were glad when they seemed happy and sad when they died.

Parakeets are not indigenous to Cyprus and had to be imported. Perhaps a few people took to the habit and others followed suit. Aficionados considered this extreme preoccupation with keeping birds quite normal. There was no such interest among the Greek community in Cyprus.

Dr. Volkan first wrote about the subject in a chapter of his book *Cyprus: War and Adaptation* printed in 1979. He recounted the following during his interviews.

> Before suggestions about the psychological meaning of this mass hobby are formulated, the symbolic meaning of birds should be touched upon. A look at folklore and mythology in connection to birds yields a great variety of symbolic meanings. I will concern myself here only with birds as a symbol of freedom in the general sense, including psychic freedom. Psychic freedom is the goal of a child's struggle to achieve individuation. In the dreams of patients undergoing psychoanalysis or psychotherapy, birds not only may represent the penis, which can "go up" like a bird, but, in symbolism

unrelated to body parts, may represent the ideational aspect of indi-viduation and freedom.

I once analyzed a young man who had the habit of going to a park near Washington's National Airport to watch airplanes (big birds) take off. Under the phallic symbolism of airplanes in flight lay, as became evident in his analysis, pre-oedipal issues concerning the struggle involved in taking off from mother earth—or gaining indi-viduation and psychic freedom. Contemporary works acknowledge this symbolism. The film *Birdman of Alcatraz* tells of a prisoner who invests in his birds his desire for freedom. Reference to a prison as "a birdcage" is common; in fact, the inmates of a local prison near my old office at the University of Virginia publish a newsletter they call *The Birdcage*. In a book for children, being "free as a bird" is poetically illustrated. This is J. M. Barrie's (1906) *Peter Pan*, and the novel has essentially the same symbolism as we have discussed. Maya Angelou (1970) calls her poignant account of black childhood and youth in an American community then wholly dominated by whites *I Know Why the Caged Bird Sings*, and uses the symbol to express very much what the bird hobby meant to the Cypriot Turks. The old concept of a bird's supposedly unfettered existence is as familiar in the Turkish idiom as in the English phrase "free as a bird." Turks have an old cus-tom of buying a caged bird and freeing it when a wish comes true or when they feel that they have been saved from some looming personal disaster.

Dr. Volkan has the notion that the birds kept by Cypriot Turks at a very difficult time for the community represented a longing for freedom. Kept in the most conspicuous parts of the house, these caged birds were a source of comfort and pleasure when they sang and when they procreated. Feel-ing rather caged themselves, the Cypriot Turks tended and celebrated their birds and hoped that one day they too would be provided for, cared for, and would have their freedom.

Vamık Volkan:

This shared hobby of raising birds provided a safety valve for mass anxiety. In their plight the Turks of Cyprus had become what could be described as helpless helpers; as long as they could help their birds to be happy and to flourish, they could entertain the hope that they themselves would one day be likewise happy and flourishing. They did not consciously think, "We are like caged birds now, but we want to be free as birds on the wing at some point," but their aspirations were expressed through what we can call a living metaphor.

The Cypriot Turks regressed under pressure. Intellectually, they knew rather well they were not birds; yet, in their distress they projected their identities onto the birds. Members of regressed groups get more dependent on external power instead of their own reasoning and give up part of their own judgement. Such a group seeks an ideal example, a leader (see Volkan, 2004).

Dr. Volkan holds that the Cypriot Turks were deprived of a leader who would save them from their plight when they were forced into enclaves. From the start of this dire period they believed that Turkey would come to their rescue. Certainly, Turkish aerial bombardment at Christmas 1963 and in August 1964 helped to stem the Greek onslaught to an extent and hopes were high that more military intervention would be forthcoming. However, Turkish efforts remained largely in the realms of politics and Turkish Cypriot dreams of a great leader in Ankara soon faded. They raised parakeets instead of hopes.

The pressure the Cypriots were under led them to an unconscious identification with the birds in a regressive manner, not in a conscious manner (Volkan, 1979). And there is another aspect to the parakeet saga, that of denial and comparison. When the birds were well fed and happy, their owners could partly deny their own plight and could nurture their love of self. When the birds sang, they seemed to praise their owners. Also, although confined to enclaves, the people concerned were a good deal freer than the birds and this comparison allowed them to feel a little less victimized.

The Greeks "allowed" the Turks to exit their enclaves in the summer of 1968. The political shift of 1968 seemed like a liberation; however, it soon proved itself to be but another form of captivity. Exiting one enclave only meant being able to enter another. True freedom to enjoy the whole island was not on offer. The fantasy world of the Cypriot Turks collapsed and finally group depression set in.

Interest in birds started to diminish a few months after this. At around this time Dr. Volkan expressed the possibility of the birds representing the captive Turks in a conference in Cyprus attended by Turkish intellectuals.

While not exactly being howled down, this assertion was not well received and Dr. Volkan realized that he had made the mistake of the "immature and untimely comment."

That same year an observant but erroneous commentator wrote that the Cypriot Turks no longer had the time or the inclination to raise parakeets because they were able to move about. He was right in one way. The birds had practically disappeared. On a visit to Cyprus in 1973, Vamık came across parakeets only in one place, at a private house. He did not see a single cage in any grocery store or other public place.

Invisible walls

Following his retirement in 2002, Dr. Volkan took to spending his summers in Northern Cyprus. After decades in America, he decided to learn a little about the experience of being a Cypriot Turk living on the island. He met many young people, most of whom were at the end of adolescence and some of whom were in their early twenties. He also met officials both in office and retired and political party workers. This was the summer of 2007 and the summer of 2008. To further comprehend the impact of decades of living in an anomalous polity with its physical and invisible walls, Dr. Volkan also took observations at family gatherings, social events, and in workplaces.

To Dr. Volkan, while writing or talking about what has been happening in Cyprus for the last fifty years, the Cypriot Greeks and the Cypriot Turks, or, as he says, "in reality generally Greeks and Turks," have tended to emphasize two different events that they deem the most traumatic and devastating for their communities. When it comes to social trauma arising from the "Cyprus Problem," the Greeks consider the Turkish Army's landing on the island in July 1974 and the de facto division of the island as by far the greatest. When the Turks talk or write about the "Cyprus Problem," they hark back to 1963 when they were expelled from the organs of state and pushed into enclaves to languish under very severe conditions for the following eleven years.

Dr. Volkan came to realize that the enclaves lingered on in symbolic form, that the psychological effects of this difficult time had not resolved themselves comfortably into the past. While resident in Charlottesville, he received a phone call from someone introducing himself as a friend of a friend from Cyprus. This person said he had set out on a world tour with his wife and daughter and that a mutual friend had insisted they should visit Vamık Volkan on the US leg of their travels. They duly flew in from Japan and landed in Florida from where the friend of a friend telephoned Dr. Volkan. He asked if the family could pay him a visit on their way to New York, where they were to catch a plane for Turkey and then another to Cyprus. Dr. Volkan said he would be delighted and two days later his guests appeared. The man, obviously rich, held forth on the wonderful globetrotting experiences the family had undergone. Dr. Volkan was curious as to how they could have found their way around the world using passports which were recognized by no country on earth bar Turkey. The man just said that the passports got them where they wanted (something Dr. Volkan rather doubted), yet became agitated on the subject. How awful to have a national identity that others didn't recognize! The anger was palpable. While Dr. Volkan did not get to the bottom of the passport logistics, the visit stayed in his mind. The man was clearly railing at the invisible walls.

Vamık Volkan:

> As I observed, the Cypriot Turks were not really dealing with the idea that they were living with a symbolic blockade in their everyday lives in the summer months of 2007. Since 1974 they have felt safe and have directed their efforts towards making money, competing with their compatriots in terms of career curve and prestige, providing for their families, educating their children, and generally behaving much as people do anywhere. The issue of being second-class citizens of the world is repressed. Having been "saved" by Turkey in 1974 was no longer a topic of conversation. Somehow this "illegal" state found, at least ostensibly, "legal" ways to become a part of the world, and its citizens became able to participate in many global activities as we see with our globetrotting man and his family.
>
> With six universities established in Northern Cyprus and with students from at least forty different countries arriving for higher education, it was hard for the citizens to think that they themselves and their TRNC identities were not recognized by the wider world community. [In 2019 the number of universities in North Cyprus has risen to thirteen with nearly 100,000 students from foreign countries, from Turkey, the Middle East, central Asia, and Africa.] Tourists also came from many different countries, traveled around the region and visited the castles, the beautiful beaches, the entertainment centers and casinos. Alas, the underlying reality of the

influx was that Northern Cyprus had become the gambling center of the Middle East.

Around this time there was a housing boom in North Cyprus. Swathes of trees were cut down, particularly near beaches and in the hills and these were replaced by concrete. Areas of outstanding natural beauty were not immune to this devastation. On the surface, this took away the shared perception of being viewed as second-class citizens. After all, this was supposedly economic progress and people came from distant lands to buy into the local lifestyle. This was an illusion. Meanwhile, the interminable political debates of local leaders and international authorities regarding the "Cyprus Problem" progressed on leaden feet. Each day saw a reaffirmation on talk shows and in newspaper columns that the country was not recognized by the outside world. The new word used by the diplomatic world to describe the invisible blockade of the Cypriot Turks was "isolation."

The work Vamık Volkan did in 2007 and 2008 gave him an insight into what he terms "forced enclave mentality." The conditions under which shared trauma was experienced passed, but the trauma did not. The enclave mentality did not. Dr. Volkan hopes that historical events and a new generation of inspirational leaders might change this lamentable aspect of the shared identity of the community. Perhaps the enclave mentality need not be around forever.

Vamık Volkan:

> During the war of 1974, some Cypriot Turks found very precious things left behind by the fleeing Cypriot Greeks. We have to call this looting. People speculated as to who had pillaged what, as to what value of loot had been dredged from the mire. And as Cypriot Turks headed for the north as part of the population exchange, leaving their homes and their lands behind, they were allocated empty Greek Cypriot properties. Settlers arrived from Turkey and they were likewise given houses belonging to Greeks. Those connected with the Turkish military were given priority. [Today, the land issue—who legally owns what land and how one can seek redress if dispossessed—is the fundamental obstacle to a solution to the Cyprus Problem.] The distribution of the booty changed the enclave mentality and society became imbued with two feelings that became widespread.

The first feeling was one of selfishness, as people became alienated from others when they found they had acquired things their relatives and neighbors did not possess and as they hugged the loot and the secret of its origin to themselves. This selfishness also manifested itself in less than sensitive behavior towards others in wider society. Slinging rubbish from cars and dumping in one's neighbors' gardens became commonplace. While tourism assets were kept clean through the profit motive, the municipalities struggled to keep even a semblance of a clean environment in the streets and in the countryside. The beaches became a disgrace. This has been the case for decades. I think this bad habit is related to memories of having lived in enclaves full of garbage. The deeper the mire, the better the loot can be hidden.

The second feeling which became prevalent in the community was envy. People who lost out in the division of spoils envied the nouveau riche. Stories proliferated of one brother becoming very wealthy and the other brother being broke. The poor brother was no longer on speaking terms with the rich brother. Thus, an emotional division was cleaved between Cypriot Turks and it extended to the mainland settlers taking up residence in deserted Greek Cypriot villages.

There was another complication which added to the identity confusion and social division. Endless efforts by Americans and Europeans to create an ethnic group on the island, to forge a new nation of Greeks and Turks living together, did not get far but raised great passions. Shortly after the events of 1974 I was called to the U.S. State Department because the people at the Cyprus Desk wanted to meet a Cypriot Turk and get some information concerning his people. At that time, I had no experience in international affairs and large-group psychology. I remember how an American diplomat who wanted to merge the Cypriot Turks and the Cypriot Greeks and to create a new nation exploded in a meeting. He said: "What's the problem with these people? Why can't they come together as a composite nation as we have in the USA?"

Official and unofficial initiatives from overseas to overcome ethnic and identity issues in Cyprus have rolled down the decades, but the fact is that there has never really been a Cypriot ethnicity or a Cypriot nation

(Ortaylı, 2007). While meeting with young Cypriot Turks in 2007 and 2008, Dr. Volkan observed that some saw "Cypriotness" as their fundamental ethnic origin. He concluded that these youngsters were in denial about their personal narratives and that they had a diminished sense of their parents as role models. Some whose grandparents had played a significant part in their upbringing and who had grown up listening to accounts of the heroic struggles of the past took a very different view of their large-group identity. It is understandable that the older generation had an exaggerated take on "Turkishness," that this should be part and parcel of the stand against the sense of humiliation and victimhood, and it is equally understandable that the younger generation should be perplexed by this, indeed partially reject it.

Because being Cypriot is often equated with being Greek, the situation is different on the other side. A Cypriot identity cannot be allowed to outweigh a Greek identity. Propaganda in this direction has met with a great deal of success (Mavratsas, 1999). The idea among many is that being Cypriot entails the Cypriot Greeks having the power and the Cypriot Turks being consigned to the status of a minority. Again, a kind of invisible enclave. Dr. Volkan believes that an attempt to forge a common identity for the Cypriot Turks and Greeks is like chasing a phantom. With all the heavy baggage of history, such an endeavor would meet with as much success as a project to create a common state for the Arabs and the Israelis.

The Annan Plan

Undeterred by local realities, the United Nations Under-Secretary-General Kofi Annan came up with a plan to lay the Cyprus Problem to rest in April 2004. It was known as the Annan Plan. In early 1999, Álvaro de Soto, a Peruvian diplomat, had become Kofi Annan's special advisor on Cyprus and so Dr. Volkan was keen to meet him when both men attended an international gathering in Peru dealing with psychoanalytical matters. Both of them were on the panel fielding questions about the psychological aspects of international affairs. Afterwards they spent some time talking about the situation in Cyprus. De Soto spoke about his family's past and impressed Vamık Volkan with his interest in and knowledge of large-group psychology. They stayed in touch by email.

When Álvaro de Soto came to Cyprus in search of a solution to the political impasse, Dr. Volkan was in residence. De Soto paid Dr. Volkan a visit in his house prior to his meeting Rauf Denktaş, president of the Turkish Republic of Northern Cyprus. Dr. Volkan asked that the president should not know of their meeting and De Soto assured him he would not burden the president with this knowledge.

Vamık Volkan:

> I had discussions with Álvaro de Soto for about two hours. He wanted to know where I stood on a possible solution to the Cyprus Problem. I told him of certain things that I considered unrealistic and I explained to him that ideas about a solution tended to pivot around the concept of "Cypriotness," and that I thought such a thing unworkable politically even if desirable as a sentiment. Instead of such a thing, I suggested the "Swiss-cheese-border" approach that I had been advocating at various academic meetings. In short, this would involve Cypriot Greeks and Cypriot Turks looking primarily after their own internal affairs while maintaining a physical border between them. This border would also function as a psychological one, a demarcation of each side's large-group identities. However, this border should have holes, like holes in a block of Swiss cheese; people belonging to political, societal, artistic, and other like organizations would be able to and be expected to pass through such "holes" and share their expertise and ideas in the interests of the island as a whole. Once the chairs were back on the tables, as it were, everyone would return to their place under his or her side's ethnic umbrella. This way there would be no space for humiliation. Such an approach would remove the Turkish side's isolation by creating a common Cypriot state with two sides existing peacefully under well-thought-out legal conditions. I knew at that time that a two state solution was not politically feasible and that such an outcome was not worth the time and effort spent in promoting it. I did not meet Álvaro de Soto again or communicate any further with him about his assignment.

Eventually, the Annan Plan was presented to the peoples as a bi-zonal, bi-communal Cyprus separated along ethnic lines, albeit rather blurred lines. Although there were elements that Dr. Volkan did not like very much, he saw it as quite similar to his Swiss cheese model. While the plan was accepted by sixty-five percent of the Cypriot Turks, it was rejected by seventy-five percent of the Cypriot Greeks. There were various reasons for the Cypriot Greeks to reject the Annan Plan, such as the great number of Turkish settlers gaining citizenship and their suspicions over whether Turkey would keep its promise about withdrawing their troops from the island (Varnava & Faustmann, 2009). With their hopes dashed, the Cypriot Turks nursed their disappointment and their pain.

Direct and indirect efforts on the part of various countries and non-governmental organizations to create a mutual Cypriot identity persisted after the failure of the Annan Plan. For example, there were initiatives to lessen hostility by revising school textbooks and their recounting of the troubles. Addressing these historical issues is a necessary prerequisite to overcoming past traumas in the older generation and to reducing the hand-down effect on the younger generation. Dr. Volkan believes that repressing and denying painful memories does not seem to be a good option. A comprehension of historical continuity (rather than hanging onto before-and-after style history) can strengthen large-group identities and allow the children of erstwhile enemies to sit down at the table of brotherhood.

Ekopolitik project

The research Dr. Volkan undertook in 2007 and 2008, as we have noted, pointed to a deficit of TRNC large-group identity among the populace. People defined themselves in various ways: a Turk; a secular Turk on the lines favored by Atatürk; a Turk who loves Turkey and sees him- or herself as an outpost of Turkdom in common with many in other parts of the world; a Turkish believer in the True Faith; a Cypriot in commonality with Cypriot Greeks; or, sadly, a very lonely individual without a large-group identity.

Needless to say, identity issues can cause a whole lot of trouble. Dr. Volkan notes that this is certainly the case at the myriad universities in North Cyprus and a cause of concern among the university authorities. For instance, it is entirely routine for Turkish Cypriot students to flock together rather than mingling with mainland Turkish students. If a Cypriot is dating a mainland Turk then he or she may be shunned. Cypriots tend to see mainland Turks as overly religious and overly nationalistic and for this reason will very often try to separate themselves from the mainlanders. Alas, this can, as put to Dr. Volkan by university staff, lead to violence.

We did some work on 4–5 June 2009 with Ekopolitik, a center for economic and social research based in Istanbul which aims to develop new policy-making opportunities for decision-making bodies. We brought influential people from among the Cypriot Turks and the mainland Turks to put their attention to current issues such as the "enclave mentality," identity confusion, societal problems in the TRNC, the problems which fester between the native Cypriot Turks and Turkish authorities in Turkey, and more importantly, to try to write out "prescriptions." I use this word to try to instill the idea that social problems are like a physical disease requiring treatment. I also use this word in a reassuring manner. No, it is not terminal. Yes, there is a remedy. Moreover, I evoked the clinical advisedly. Just as one does not look down on someone who has contracted an illness, so one should not look down on people who are living with societal malaise. Cypriot Turks do not need others to take a "What the hell is wrong with you?" attitude towards them.

Turkey may have saved the Turks of Cyprus in 1974, but the "mainland" is no longer perceived as a good parent. Turkey, adopting the role of a good parent after the intervention, wanted its child to grow up and take responsibility for itself despite the fact that its child was traumatized due to having been living in "invisible enclaves." We have touched on identity issues and perhaps we now stress that better relations between Cypriot Turks and the mainland would ameliorate these things. Fragmentation of society on the island can be addressed with a better mutual understanding and a greater level of respect between the islanders and the mainlanders. This is not a matter to be dealt with by harping back to Greco-Turkish issues and for this reason I decided to put this aspect of the Cyprus Problem out of bounds in our discussions.

We numbered sixteen in the meeting and this included a representative from the TRNC presidential office, former and current members of parliament including the former TRNC foreign affairs minister, the former TRNC chief justice, the head of the Religious Administration Bureau, academics, and journalists.

Held in June 2009, this meeting is generally thought to be seminal. First behind closed doors and later in the public arena, we aired ideas from ways in which we could reach a better and more sensitive approach to Cyprus on the part of the Turkish authorities to the psychology of Cypriot Turks litterbugging, flytipping, and generally fouling their own nest.

When I talked to Dr. Volkan in August 2014 he believed that the identity confusion and the collective angst of the Cypriot Turks were less pronounced than they were in 2007 and 2008.

CHAPTER TEN

Linking objects, linking phenomena, and nostalgia in large groups

With Yasser Arafat in Tunis, Tunisia, 1990.

In 1972, Dr. Volkan outlined two concepts that he termed "linking objects" and "linking phenomena" (see also Volkan, 1981). These refer to the tools people use in the complicated mourning process.

People who are mourning struggle with their internal relationship with the departed. This struggle might sometimes lead to different results in terms of personal and environmental reasons that we cannot describe here. What is important is what people in mourning do with these mental images related to the lost person or object.

A result of mourning is the mourner's healthy and selective identification with the mental images of the lost object. And this allows the person's self-representation to become richer, because the functions carried out by the lost person or object can now be carried out by the mourner himself.

Mourning takes a different direction when the mourner identifies with the total mental representation of a person departed, to which the mourner had related with severe ambivalence. As a result of this non-selective identification, the mourner identifies with both the liked and the disliked characteristics of the lost object. In consequence, the self-representation of the mourning person turns into a war between love and hate. The mourner gets trapped in ambivalent feelings directed at the self and, as such, might experience depression.

Complications in one's mourning process do not always lead to depression, but may result in another outcome, called "established pathological mourning." Adults suffering from this become "perennial mourners," doomed to remain preoccupied with aspects of their mourning process for decades to come and even until the end of their own lives. Perennial mourners experience their mourning without bringing it to a practical conclusion. There are various degrees of severity in such a condition. Some perennial mourners live miserable lives. Others express their unending mourning in more creative ways, but even then, most of these people, when not obsessed with their creativity, feel uncomfortable.

The following is a description of the internal world of a perennial mourner: To a large degree, the mourner cannot identify with the selected enriching aspects of the object representation of the lost item. On the other hand, the mourner does not end up identifying totally with the object representation of the same. In other words, the mourner cannot go through a "normal" mourning process or cannot slide into depression. Instead, the mourner keeps the object images of the lost person or thing within his or her self-representation as specific and *unassimilated* "foreign bodies."

Technically such a foreign body is called an "introject." The ambivalent relationship of the past continues in the mourner's involvement with the introject; the mourner is torn between a strong yearning for the restored presence of the lost person or thing and an equally deep dread that the lost item might be confronted. The presence of the introject provides an illusion of choice and, in this way, it reduces anxiety. But, having an introject also means the continuation of an internal struggle with it. Some feel as if another person is present inside them.

A man came to see Dr. Volkan complaining that his younger brother had been disturbing him daily and he did not know how to deal with the situation. He sought treatment in order to free himself from his brother's influence. He explained that while driving to work in his car his brother constantly talked with him, even when Dr. Volkan's patient wanted some time for himself or when he wanted to listen to the car radio. His brother gave him advice about everything. For example, he made suggestions as to how the patient should behave when meeting his boss or when talking to a particular secretary at work. The patient did not like his brother's advice. Sometimes he told his brother to shut up, but the younger man continued to talk and irritate him. Dr. Volkan also learned that when both men were young the patient had experienced considerable sibling rivalry.

In his mind, Dr. Volkan pictured his patient in his car with his brother sitting next to him. He even imagined that his patient and the patient's brother lived together in the same house or at least nearby, which would explain their riding together each workday to the downtown business area. Therefore, Dr. Volkan was really surprised when his patient, in his sixth therapeutic session, informed him that his younger brother had died six years before in an accident. The "brother" with whom he had conversations while driving to work was actually his brother's unassimilated object representation. The patient felt it to be lodged in his chest. Sometimes he experienced this object representation as a puppet-sized younger brother sitting on one of his shoulders, literally a symbolized burden on his shoulder. But most of the time, the "brother" was inside the patient's body image. The patient carried on his internal conversations with his brother's introject.

A linking object is the externalized form of an introject. People in a state of perennial mourning will choose an external object such as a father's watch and render that object magical to them. Linking objects are living or nonliving objects that unconsciously link the mental representation of the lost person or object with the self-representation of the person concerned, and this prepares a mutual psychological meeting ground between the two. Sometimes this can ease the mind of the mourner and quell internal struggles.

As for the linking phenomenon (the name given to links that are not physical objects), it can be a song, a scent, a gesture, or any given sensation serving as a linking object.

Vamık Volkan:

> For instance, a woman who says it was raining at her father's funeral and the song "Raindrops Keep Falling on My Head" played internally told me that whenever she felt a need to address her mourning process, she used this song as a linking phenomenon.

While talking about the mourning process with Dr. Volkan, he and I realized that he had been exposed to the utilization of linking objects when he was a child. As is written in Chapter Three, Vamık Volkan's maternal grandmother had kept items belonging to her dead son Ömer Vamık. She and Vamık's mother used these items as their linking objects. We also noted that the President Rauf Denktaş' wife was also holding onto her linking objects in her unending mourning for losing her daughter. Later, Dr. Volkan would see how using linking objects was part of the history of the Palestine Liberation Organization (PLO).

The Palestine Liberation Organization

Following an Israeli offensive and Phalangist atrocities in the Sabra and Shatila refugee camps, the PLO agreed to relocate to Tunisia and it was there that Vamık Volkan met the leadership and others in the organization. He was particularly interested in how nostalgia was used in bonding within a large group.

> In the spring of 1990, I spent ten days in Tunisia in order to see children living in a Palestinian orphanage called Biet Atfal Al-Sommound. This orphanage, managed by the PLO, was not far away from the headquarters of this organization in Tunis and a good percentage of Palestinians including Yasser Arafat lived there at this time

before the subsequent relocation to the West Bank. Security was uppermost in the minds of my hosts; they constantly feared Israeli commando attacks. It was said Arafat did not stay in one place for long but moved around a great deal. Anxiety was ever present. The Palestinians there felt exiled and longed to return to their lands under conditions of peace and stability. Despite the fact that the Tunisian government gave the PLO full autonomy, almost all the Palestinians considered themselves refugees in Tunisia.

The orphanage housed fifty-two children who had lost one or both of their parents in the Middle East conflict. The PLO granted permission to Dr. Volkan and two Americans of Palestinian descent, one a psychiatrist and one a psychologist, to spend time with these children and work on the psychology of war orphans.

Vamık Volkan:

> Although we had received permission to visit the orphanage beforehand, they made us wait for three days when we reached Tunisia, probably so they could vet us. Many children in the orphanage were named Arafat because their fathers' names were unknown. It was said the leader, Yasser Arafat, often spent time in the orphanage and sent gifts to the kids. This was the time of the intifada, the largely unarmed Palestinian uprising against the Israelis, and the children in the orphanage would spontaneously burst into song, recounting their victimhood and identifying with the children of the intifada they had seen on television. They often expressed their hopes and desires to return to a "Free Palestine."
>
> I was asked on one of my visits why I wasn't planning on interviewing Palestinians older than eighteen. I replied that the focus had been on children since the start of the project and I had not wished to deviate from this. That said, I expressed a willingness to interview an adult if one would come forward. At lunch with senior PLO leaders, I met a young woman in her twenties. She asked me if I could interview her to which I said, yes, I certainly could. She introduced herself (in perfect English) as the daughter of a hijacker. When she was still a child, her father had hijacked a plane and forced it to land in Israel where he demanded the release of some Palestinian

prisoners. She held that Israeli forces had tricked her father, then shot him dead.

Although she allowed her real name to be used, Vamık Volkan declines to do so.

> Hers is a story of an upbringing pivoting around the "hero ghost"— that is, the mental representation of her father. After her father's death, most of his friends in high places in the PLO treated her as a very special person, a martyr's daughter and a symbol of Palestine. More materially, they helped with her education. She subsequently became Yasser Arafat's secretary and thereby attended many social and official meetings of the leadership and accompanied them on various trips. This young woman felt the need to remain an untouchable flower, as it were, in the midst of the bloody Arab–Israeli conflict that has ever been the backdrop to her life. As our interview drew to an end, I asked her why she had come to our hotel late in the night, of her own accord, and unburdened her fears and desires to a complete stranger. She told me she had the role of a "flag" for the Palestinians living in Tunisia and that she also knew she was flesh and blood. She dreamt of finding a partner and getting married—that is, of being an ordinary person.
>
> In fact, what she wanted was to be both a symbol of her people and an ordinary woman, but she also realized that in order to be the one she had to give up the other. Seeing no immediate solution to this dilemma, she started to daydream about losing both of these roles. She imagined being on a plane with Arafat (her hero/father figure) which exploded in mid-air killing them both. Psychoanalysts may infer other meanings to her daydream, such as a wish for reunion with her dead father image, but here I simply want to stick with her inner struggle to be a symbol or a regular woman.
>
> Historians writing about the PLO will probably never mention this young woman's role in Tunisia from the end of the 1980s to the start of the 1990s. Maybe some will understand the need of a people living in conditions of conspiracy, violence, and death, experiencing high levels of anxiety, to have a "living linking object" representing their longings. Using this woman as a representative,

as an idealization of their people, may have eased the pain of exile and kept alive the hope that they would return. This young woman was an untouchable virgin, a living linking object for Palestinians in Tunisia. She nurtured her sense of purity as a defense mechanism in the face of so much of the opposite and she let herself be an embodiment of Palestinian hopes of a brighter future.

Dr. Volkan is reminded of the parakeets in Cyprus touched upon above. Cypriot Turks have also found ways of keeping hope alive.

CHAPTER ELEVEN

Immigration, globalization, and racism

When social cohesion breaks down, or when there are conflicts threatening the social order of a polity, problems arise for "the other" living within the legally defined borders of a large group. As we have seen time and again over the last few decades in places such as the former Yugoslavia, Georgia, the Middle East, and many others, notably sub-Saharan Africa, many are forced to leave their homes, their communities, their familiar surroundings, and to try to make a new life elsewhere. That conflict be left behind and not be replicated in the new host country must be the hope of most involuntary migrants. Engineering peaceful coexistence is a task which falls both to the migrants and the hosts. The latter may have to adopt new approaches and perceptions of their large-group identity and this may entail bold sociopolitical initiatives. Sometimes inclusiveness can result in what is often called a rainbow nation. Sometimes nationalism and her ugly sister racism rear their heads.

I interviewed Dr. Volkan about immigration in 2013 before the establishment of ISIS, the so-called Islamic State of Iraq and the Levant, and millions of Syrians escaping to other locations. What I present here, however, tells us about the psychology of immigrants and refugees anywhere. In 2017 Dr. Volkan published a book on this topic. He says that in order to get to grips with problems attendant on a refugee influx, data from different disciplines is required.

My visits to Georgia and Croatia in the late 1990s, combined with what I had observed in North Cyprus much earlier, taught me a great deal about the psychology of internally displaced persons (IDPs) and refugees. This led me to compare the internal worlds of involuntary and voluntary migrants. I was a voluntary immigrant myself when I came to the United States. I have seen and contrasted myself with involuntary migrants, some of them extensively such as IDPs in Tbilisi and some briefly such as those in Zagreb. The internal worlds of voluntary immigrants are vastly different from those of IDPs, refugees, and asylum seekers. Nevertheless, there are also common elements that underlie the psychology of both the voluntary immigrant and the traumatized forced migrant. Moving from a familiar to an unfamiliar place, the sense of loss of home, loss of familiar faces, language, music, dances, food, indeed smells, is not easy to adjust to. The dislocation experienced involves the need to mourn these losses, the need to cope with external and internal adjustment. Also, the by no means easy task of learning another language in many cases.

In cases of "voluntary" immigration [this word is put in inverted commas as there are degrees of consent] the dislocated tend to have a smoother path to integration into the adopted polity—as long as the individual's psychology allows this. I came to the United States voluntarily to expand my medical training with the idea that I would return to Cyprus when I had finished my studies. This was anticipated to be a few short years, but sixty years on and here I still am. Certain events in my life led me to become an American citizen.

It is clear that individuals make their decision to settle in a new location for myriad reasons. At the beginning there is, to one degree or another, culture shock for all dislocated individuals. The voluntary migrant tends to have a positive image of the past, with mostly good memories getting through the filter. As the new reality of their current situation sets in, they will often miss the people and places and sensations of their past lives even if the positive images are largely a fantasy.

Advances in information technology and globalization have ameliorated culture shock these days, but by no means eradicated it. But with the right approach to mourning the past, a settler in an unfamiliar country can surmount this.

A refugee, an involuntary migrant, can find greater difficulty in overcoming this problem. Mourning and getting over culture shock can be more protracted.

Vamık Volkan:

> The migrant might yearn for the things which are left behind while showing little inclination to find good things in the new environment. For those who have fled severe persecution or genocide so much the worse. They may have trouble in developing nostalgic fantasies of the land left behind due to an unconscious fear that imagining such things will mean that they too are destroyed. This can leave the person in a very poor psychological state in which he or she feels no continuity and no positive links with the new polity.
>
> This being so, we can still point to incidences of successful integration into a new society on the part of survivors of atrocity. There are many psychological mechanisms that help recovery. How much a person is welcomed into a new society is pivotal here, along with how much opportunity there is to visit the old homeland and how rapidly the individual concerned is able to master the intricacies of a new language.

Salman Akhtar (2010) suggests immigration initiates a "third individuation." The first individuation occurs in childhood when children take their first steps towards finding their own individuality. The second individuation occurs in adolescence when the images of people and objects that were important to the teenager back in childhood are unconsciously reviewed. Some images are left as they are, while others are revised and adolescents change their internal worlds and identities and add images from their expanding worlds. The third individuation occurs in migrants when they allow themselves to experience a biculturalism, whereby they belong neither to the old nor to the new culture—but instead internalize aspects of both—but exclude neither.

Along with Dr. Volkan's research, his personal experience in this regard is also important. He recounts his relationship with Demetrios Julius, the psychiatrist and sleep specialist in Richmond, Virginia.

Referring to his own experiences, Demetrios explained how he slowly came to appreciate the importance of intrapsychic cultural complementarity. As he reached an acceptance of the vast cultural differences between the two countries foremost in his life (Greece and the United States), he said he "began to accept certain psychological paradoxes and feel myself truly bicultural" [Julius, 1992, p. 56]. My own experiences are almost identical to Demetrios'. Nonetheless, he has no foreign accent when he speaks English and I do. Also, after living in the United States for so long, I have an altered accent when I speak Turkish. This sometimes creates uncomfortable situations in which I am treated as an "other." On many occasions in recent years, while shopping or ordering meals at a restaurant in Turkey, a shopkeeper or waiter will ask me, "Where did you study Turkish? How did you learn to speak it so well?" I always answer, "I had no choice. My mother taught me how to speak Turkish."

If children settle into a new country prior to their second individuation without external complications, their adjustment to and assimilation of the new culture will be, generally, easier. They will learn how to speak the new language without a foreign accent. However, adult immigrants, with or without being aware of it, pass on to their children aspects of traditions and history that had supposedly been left behind. As Ernst Kris stated long ago, "Under the disguise of full compliance with the new environment, cultural heritages of the past, though attenuated by time and intermarriage, live on among men" [1975, p. 467].

In 1993 we held a conference at CSMHI in Charlottesville on the topic of immigrants and refugees. One of the participants was Howard Stein, an anthropologist of European Jewish ancestry who was born in the United States. Among his works was his study of the Slovak and Russian experience in the Steel Valley of western Pennsylvania. For this study, he visited many Slovak and Russian homes. One day he realized that all the interviews were taking place in the kitchen and occasionally an adjacent dining room. He felt uneasy because in the culture in which he had been raised visitors were made comfortable in the living room. Then he learned that in the Slavic world, the kitchen was the room of choice when receiving visitors, a place where family and friends could relax, eat, and drink. Traditions had been passed from generation to generation and across frontiers. Only priests, politicians, dignitaries, and suchlike guests were brought into the formal living room.

Howard Stein's research also touched on prejudice against "the other" as people crossed frontiers and sought new objects of disdain. Slovaks and Russians in Eastern Europe tended to despise Jews and gypsies as a means of throwing themselves into positive relief. Once in the USA a new group to look down upon was found. In the United States, despised and envied out-groups helped define Slovak and Russian identities.

Howard Stein writes,

> To a degree, the role of Jews and Gypsies as outcasts in Eastern Europe was transferred to blacks in the United States. Blacks became the new out-group embodying the bad counter-image to Slovaks and Russians, whose positive self-image was that of industriousness, thrift, generosity, friendliness, nonviolence, and sexual probity. At the same time, immigrant Slovaks and Russians were themselves stigmatized by more mainstream Americans who were anxious about their own social standing as "real" Americans. They lumped Slovaks, Russians, Magyars, Croats, Serbs, Slovenians, Macedonians, and others into a single degrading image, that of "Hunkies," whom they characterized as stupid, fat, brutal, drunk, and only suitable for hard labor. (1993, p. 87)

Forced immigration entails trauma associated with fear for one's life, survival guilt, humiliation, helplessness, the aftermath of torture, and so on. When the sense of loss attendant on dislocation is put in as an admixture to this painful cocktail, it can be very difficult for IDPs and refugees to undergo effective mourning in their exile and for this reason, they find it impossible to adapt to their new situations.

> Immigrants use linking objects as perennial mourners do. Their investment in such objects is withdrawn slowly as their adjustment to the new environment occurs and as they begin to feel comfortable with biculturalism. Two or three years after I arrived in the United States and began to feel that this country would be my permanent home, I collected pictures of my parents, sisters, other relatives,

friends, and myself back in Cyprus and I made an album. On the cover I wrote: "My life before I came to America." At the time I had no idea why I had made such an album. After I became a psychoanalyst, I realized that this album was my linking object. I still keep it somewhere, but it has lost its original emotional power. I wrote earlier about how I kept the newspaper clipping that announced the murder of Erol, my roommate from my medical school days in Ankara [Volkan, 2013]. This newspaper clipping is also a linking object. Both the album and the clipping are personal items; they only belong to me and they only have emotional meaning for me.

Vamık Volkan worked with a family at Tbilisi Sea near the city of Tbilisi in Georgia from May 1998 to March 2002. They had a linking object and it was alive. It was a dog resident in their rather squalid and overcrowded apartment and it had a special place therein. When this family had to flee Abkhazia in terror of their lives, they could not take their dog with them. Once at Tbilisi Sea, where they settled, they came across a dog similar to the one they had left behind. They adopted it and gave it the same name as their former pet. To Dr. Volkan, this dog was seen as a means of connecting with the familiar places of the past and was also a symbol of what had been lost—and at the same time a symbol of rebirth in a new environment.

The family were the proud owners of a yellow telephone, which was the only phone possessed by any of the people—some 3,000 or so—who had been forced out of their homes and had ended up at the Tbilisi Sea. Mobile phones were yet to come and all of these internally displaced people had but this one yellow telephone to connect them with the places and people they had left behind. A small, unprepossessing linking object. Just as with the kitchens of Slovak and Russian émigrés in Pennsylvania mentioned earlier.

Internal migrants were settled in and around Tbilisi, as we have seen, yet the troubles were not over for these victims of oppression. Before long signs went up in their adopted region with the main drift being "Refugees Go Home." The city was now going through an apparent schism. Some of the IDPs were seen as heroes. Some were teachers, some respected artists, writers, and athletes. However, this provided no immunity as a majority of the natives of this region, in spite of being ethnically no different, decided that the newcomers would ruin their economy and pose a physical threat. However, passions died down after a while and no great disaster occurred.

Members of a large group can also become refugees without leaving their environment. When they are restricted in their movements, when relatives and friends are killed, the people concerned are alienated from their familiar environment without exiting it. Dr. Volkan cites Palestine as an example here:

> When the Israelis bulldozed Palestinians' houses, the former residents would keep the keys. These keys began to symbolize the reality of their loss and the hope of restitution. As time passed, the symbol of a key became a shared linking object and also the symbol of Palestinian identity. Palestinian politicians began coming to international meetings with a picture of a key pinned to their coat lapels.
>
> As the twenty-first century approached, some felt that Europe was on the verge of an unprecedented era of social, economic, and political cooperation. It was, after all, around half a century since the Second World War had ravaged the continent. Moreover, the Iron Curtain had melted and the former client states of the Soviet Union were eager to join a united Europe. However, as old enmities between nation states faded and borders became more porous, there were signs that all was not well in Europe. In Eastern Europe, many fragments of the old Soviet Empire and its sphere of influence disintegrated into ethnic violence and even into genocidal warfare. There was an abundance of resurgent racism and xenophobia in Western Europe. These phenomena were primarily due to new ethnic minorities resident in places where they were often vilified, and to the many dislocated persons and asylum seekers who had come to Europe from many other parts of the world both legally and illegally. In Western Europe these minorities faced discrimination, unemployment, and poor housing, intrusive identity checks, threatening phone calls, attacks by racist gangs, bombings, beatings, murders, and the desecration of graves. The police reported 7,000 racist incidents in 1989 in London alone.

Racist theories gained a pseudoscientific gloss when Charles Darwin published *On the Origin of Species* in 1859. Darwin formed many theories on social relationships to support biological evolution. Unfortunately, "social Darwinism" resulted. Survival of the fittest has, in Darwinian terms, meant evolution by natural selection. This is a process over hundreds of millions of years. It has nothing to do with the social dispositions of contemporary humans in the tiny window of time in which we live. Dr. Volkan laments the fact that white supremacists and their ilk think it does. Racist opinions have often been expressed as if they were scientific facts.

> After my education in Ankara and after I arrived in the USA and after I completed my internship in Chicago, Illinois and my psychiatry education in Chapel Hill, North Carolina, I worked in Cherry Hospital in Goldsboro in North Carolina for about two years. In those days, Cherry Hospital was segregated. It only catered for African American patients. It was just under fifty years before an African American, Barack Obama, would become the president of the United States. I found a chance to observe racism close up at Cherry Hospital. (For more on this topic, see Volkan, 2009.)

What Dr. Volkan observed in the 1990s and 2000s in Europe is what we can call "neo-racism." Dr. Volkan states that the term "neo-racism" was created to define the situation emerging in the 1990s in Western Europe. He emphasizes that it involves hatred directed more towards perceived cultural characteristics than towards genetically determined characteristics.

In the 1950s and 1960s, West Germany, Greece, Turkey, Morocco, Portugal, Tunisia, and Yugoslavia signed an agreement to gather workers from outside their countries to work in industry. These foreigners coming to Germany to work were named *Gastarbeiter* (guest workers). In 1973 there were more than one million such workers in Germany. The foreigners began to work also in other Western European countries and to bring their families and children to join them. Dr. Volkan tells of Turkish people becoming targets of racism:

> In the 1990s Turks joined the many who were targets of neo-racism. In 1993 Gündüz Aktan, then the Turkish permanent representative to the United Nations in Geneva, approached me and CSMHI and offered to sponsor us to form a CSMHI committee to study the psychology of Western European neo-racism. He felt that it was important to have a report on the psychology of racism at a time

when the United Nations was dealing with its political, societal, and legal aspects. I formed a CSMHI committee from its members and invited some guests. Among the participants were people from Turkey, Germany, Russia, and Ghana. (To read more on this topic, see Thomson et al., 1995.)

The committee met regularly over many months. We studied the European Parliament's and the UN's reports, newspaper accounts of neo-racist incidents, theoretical and especially psychoanalytical papers about how prejudice and racism evolve in individuals, the psychology of perpetrators and victims, and psychological mechanisms that trigger violence. Our report was presented to the office of the Turkish Permanent Representative to the United Nations in Geneva and was distributed to officials dealing with neo-racism problems in Western Europe. I cannot say to what extent the CSMHI's report played a role in the official handling of this serious issue, but I know that Ambassador Aktan insisted on our conclusion that the seemingly inevitable spread of racial prejudice does not mean submission to it.

The CSMHI committee's work was one of the reasons we welcomed the study of societal issues in the Blackwell District of Richmond, Virginia in the late 1990s. The inhabitants, mainly African Americans, know this district as Southside, Richmond. Crime and drug use were rife. The Massey Foundation, also located in Richmond and a donor to the CSMHI from the outset, wanted us to get to know the Blackwell community and its religious leaders, teachers, and the Richmond city authorities. They asked us to consult with them in their efforts to make Blackwell a better place for its inhabitants and especially to prevent its young people from turning to drug use and criminality. CSMHI faculty member Maurice Apprey led this project and I accompanied him to Blackwell and Richmond city offices on several occasions.

At this time there was work available in Blackwell. Residents would wake up in the morning to the smell of tobacco in the air and this smell guided them to work in the tobacco factories. Then a catastrophic change took place. A new highway system was built around the city, shifting the sewer lines. Now, instead of smelling tobacco and knowing it was time to go to work nearby, they smelled sewage and knew it was time to figure out how to get to work in another part of town where their jobs had been relocated. This was easier said than done, as we learned one day when we examined the city bus lines on a map. We discovered that an "invisible border" had been erected around Blackwell, making it difficult to get in and out of this district. We took the map to the Richmond city officials who seemed surprised to see how Blackwell had become isolated. They were cooperative and serious about working with us to find a solution as to how to integrate Blackwell's community into the wider city. One small initiative on our part was to buy quite a fine bus with CSMHI funds to be used by teachers to break through the invisible wall and to take kids to Richmond museums and sporting events and so on.

Dr. Volkan is reminded of the invisible walls of Cyprus, the "invisible enclave."

CHAPTER TWELVE

Intergenerational transmissions, chosen traumas, and entitlement ideologies

Attending an election rally in Dakar, Senegal, 1992.

At Enver Hoxha's grave in Tirana, Albania, 1998.

Visiting Joseph Stalin's private train, with J. Anderson Thomson and Nodar Sharjveladze, at the Stalin Museum in Gori, Republic of Georgia, 2000.

When he was telling me about his being a replacement child (see Chapter Three) Dr. Volkan focused on how an adult can unconsciously deposit his or her damaged self-image onto a child with an unconscious desire to ease the pain of trauma thereby. What we can call "depositing" is closely related to the identification that takes place in childhood. It is also different in some respects. With identification, the child is active in assimilating an adult's images and ego and superego functions. With depositing, it is the adult who pushes his or her self- and object images and some related tasks onto the child. In other words, the adult uses the child as a reservoir for the adult's self-images and object images without the background that created these images. The child cannot comprehend the mental images or participate in this nonconsensual transference. Of course, memories cannot be transferred from one person to another, but an adult can deposit his or her traumatized self- and object images onto a child's self-representation. Melanie Klein's (1946) "projective identification" can explain such a process. However, Dr. Volkan uses the expression "depositing" to illustrate how parenting creates a psychological DNA (as it were) within the child.

In large-group psychology, depositing refers to a process shared by thousands or millions that starts in childhood and becomes like shared psychological DNA, creating a sense of belonging. After experiencing a collective catastrophe inflicted by an enemy, affected individuals are left with self-images similar (though not identical) to others in the group who have shared the traumatic experience. Individuals deposit such images onto their children and give them tasks such as "Regain my self-esteem for me," "Put my mourning process on the right track," or "Be assertive and take revenge." It is this transgenerational conveyance of long-term "tasks" that perpetuates the cycle of societal trauma. Thus, if the child in the second generation cannot effectively fulfill these shared tasks—and this is usually the case—he or she will pass these tasks on to the third generation and so on.

According to Vamık Volkan, depending on external conditions, shared tasks may change from generation to generation. For example, in one generation the shared task might be to grieve for their ancestors' losses and to feel their victimization, while in the following generation the shared task may be to take revenge. But whatever its expression in any given generation, keeping alive the mental double of the ancestors' trauma remains the core task. The mental representation of the event becomes the identity determinant of the large group and as time passes may turn into "chosen trauma" (Volkan, 1991, 1997, 2013).

Chosen trauma is the shared mental image of the large group's real and fantasized and even mythologized historical event which, as it is transmitted from one generation to the other, undergoes a change of function and becomes a significant large-group identity marker. This term does not apply to rather recent shared traumas at the hand of the other that still induce intense personalized feelings in people. For example, the Holocaust is not a chosen trauma. Survivors' pictures and some belongings are still at the descendants' homes, survivors' stories are still "alive." Since Jewish people were the victims of the Holocaust, this horrible historical event is a marker of their shared identity. A chosen trauma is a different type of marker of large-group identity; it is an image which has gone through a change of function, which has become connected to one degree or other with an "entitlement ideology" (Volkan, 1997). Entitlement ideologies refer to a shared sense of entitlement to recover what was lost in reality and fantasy during the ancestors' collective trauma that evolved as a chosen trauma and during other related, shared traumas. Holding onto an entitlement ideology primarily reflects a complication in large-group mourning throughout generations, an attempt both to deny losses as well as a wish to recover them, a narcissistic reorganization accompanied by "bad" prejudice for the other.

There are many other well-established chosen traumas. Orthodox Jews still refer to the 586 BC destruction of the Jewish temple in Jerusalem by Nebuchadnezzar II of Babylon; the Russians recall the "memory" of the Tartar–Mongol invasion centuries ago; Czechs commemorate the 1620 battle of Bila Hora, which led to their subjugation by the Hapsburg Empire for nearly 300 years; and Scots keep alive the story of the Battle of Culloden of 1746. Some chosen traumas are difficult to detect because they are not simply connected to one well-recognized historical event. For example, the Estonians' chosen trauma is not related to one specific event, but to the fact that they have lived under almost constant domination at the hands of Swedes, Germans, and Russians for many centuries.

Certain religious events are also utilized as chosen traumas. One might say that the crucifixion of Jesus Christ could be considered a very special and very major chosen trauma for Christians. For Shi'ites, the Battle of Karbala that took place in 680 (year 61 of the Islamic calendar) has the utmost significance in the Shi'ites' religious large-group identity. It was during this battle that Husain, a son of the fourth caliph, Ali ibn Abi Talip and grandson of the Prophet Mohammed, together with his family and followers, were deprived of water and killed upon the desert plain by soldiers of Yezid, a claimant of the caliphate. Shi'ites believe that after the death of Mohammed in 632, leadership of the Islamic faith fell to Ali ibn Abi Talip, Husain's father. This did not go smoothly, however, and when he was finally proclaimed caliph, his rule was opposed by Mu'awiyah ibn Sufyan. Ali was succeeded by his son Hasan, whom Shi'ites believe was poisoned by Mu'awiyah, who then became caliph. Husain reportedly had refused to pledge his allegiance to him and was attempting to lead his family to safety when he was attacked by Mu'awiyah's son Yezid in Karbala. As a chosen trauma, Shi'ites relive this historical atrocity on the anniversary of the Battle of Karbala.

Those Westerners who are interested in present-day Iran's internal and external affairs need to study the psychological influence this Shi'ite chosen trauma has on the Iranian large group's social, cultural, and political processes.

In Turkey, the psychiatrist Mehmet Akif Ersoy [1998] has analyzed the Alavi population in Turkey and their chosen traumas. People of the Alavi faith, a sect of Islam, are followers of the fourth caliph, Ali, but they differentiate themselves from Shi'ites. Anatolian Alavis have occasionally been excluded by the Sunnis since the early Ottoman Empire. Their hero is the folk poet and religious leader, Pir Sultan Abdal. Pir Sultan Abdal lived in the sixteenth century and was killed by Sunni Ottoman forces. This incident is a chosen trauma for Turkey's Alavis and they try to keep Pir Sultan Abdal "alive." Interestingly, the Alavis of Turkey also have Karbala as a chosen trauma.

Ersoy writes:

> I suppose that the traumatic events that the Alavis of Anatolia experienced, as well as their historical proximity to Shi'ites, have played an essential role in the acceptance and adoption of Shi'ite cultural norms such as a preoccupation with Karbala and its incorporation as an Alavi chosen trauma. (1998, p. 49)

Affective aspects of some chosen traumas may remain dormant, and some chosen traumas may only be recalled during anniversaries. However, those that become strongly connected with "entitlement ideologies" are prone to reactivation by emotions, and play a significant role in large-group social, political, and military affairs.

Each large group's entitlement ideology is specific. Some entitlement ideologies are known by specific names in the literature. What Italians call "irredentism" (related to *Italia irredenta*), what Greeks call the "Megali Idea" (or Great Idea), what Turks call "pan-Turanism" (bringing all the Turkic people together from Anatolia to central Asia), what Serbs call "Christoslavism," and what extreme religious Islamists of today call "the return of an Islamic Empire," are examples of entitlement ideologies. Such ideologies may last for centuries and may disappear and reappear when historical circumstances change and chosen traumas are activated.

They contaminate diplomatic negotiations. They may result in changing the world map in peaceful or, unfortunately too often, dreadful ways.

The Megali Idea

Vamık Volkan wrote:

> Looking at the crusades and the fall of Constantinople, Norman Itzkowitz and I have studied extensively Christian large group entitlement ideologies which have routed throughout the centuries leading up to the fall of Constantinople (today's Istanbul) to the Turks in 1453 and how, as a consequence, the Megali Idea came into being. (Volkan & Itzkowitz, 1994)

In the year AD 1071, the Seljuk Turk leader Alparslan I comprehensively defeated the Byzantine forces led by the emperor Romanus IV Diogenes near Manzikert in Eastern Anatolia. From this time on, Asia Minor gradually came to be turkified. A short while after this battle, a group of Seljuk Turks captured Jerusalem. This was the spark that set off the Crusades. It also sparked bitter enmity between the Turks and the Christians.

According to Dr. Volkan, 300 years after the Battle of Manzikert, the conquest of Constantinople by the Turks created a very clear chosen trauma in the Christian world. Constantinople was conquered by the Ottomans, successors of the Seljuks on May 29, 1453. Historically, this event marks the end of an era where the Christian Byzantine Empire was replaced by the Muslim-dominated Ottoman Empire. Because Constantinople was conquered on a Tuesday, some Christians would from then on regard Tuesday as an unpropitious day.

Vamık Volkan:

> About the capture of Constantinople by the Turks, it was said that "It is a reflection of God's judgement upon the sins of Christians everywhere" [Schwoebel, 1967, p. 14]. During the medieval and early modern ages in Europe, such recorded historical events were always associated with God's hand, thus partially denying the actual reasons for them. This mindset is by no means only a thing of long past ages. For instance, Christian fundamentalist

groups in America interpreted the tragedy of September 11 as a divine punishment for the sinful acts of homosexuals, feminists, and libertarians.

Despite the fact that Rome had ignored the Byzantines' earnest and increasingly desperate entreaties for military aid against the Turks, the fall of Constantinople was greeted with shock and disbelief in the Eternal City. The Turkish victory was regarded as a stab in the heart of Christianity. Aeneas Piccolonini, a papal candidate, wrote to Pope Nicholas IV on July 12, 1453 that the Turks had killed Homer and Plato for the second time (Schwoebel, 1967).

Dr. Volkan has it that for many in the Christian world the loss of Constantinople was a mass trauma compounding that of the loss of Jerusalem, causing shame, humiliation, and despair. Noises were made about mounting another crusade, but nothing was done in this direction. Roger Crowley writes, "The powers of Europe were too jealous, too disunited—and in some senses too secular—ever to combine in the name of Christendom again" (2005, p. 242). The bare idea of another crusade persisted, however, and the mantra was to the effect that both cities would be "ours" again in the fullness of time. Thus, the seeds were planted of a kind of ideology of entitlement to the holy cities which grew over the coming years (Young, 1969).

Vamık Volkan:

According to Niyazi Berkes [1975], a Cypriot-born famous sociologist (who was a relative of mine), there was an element of nemesis for the Turks resultant in their capture of Constantinople and indeed, their much earlier capture of Jerusalem. The Turks became the unconsciously chosen target of stubborn, systematic, and negative stereotyping by Europeans and historians throughout the West. Berkes claims that these historians never stereotyped other peoples such as the Chinese, Arabs, and Japanese in this way. Of course, since September 11, 2001, Arabs have become the main target of stereotyping in the United States. Indeed, after this tragedy President George W. Bush referred to the mental representation of the Crusades, echoing a "time collapse" of a Muslim–Christian clash of the past into a Muslim–Christian clash of the present.

As Europeans began discovering new regions of the world and colonizing them, their preoccupation with the Turks as the conquerors of Jerusalem and Constantinople became globalized. In 1539, for example, Mexico's indigenous people took part in a pageant representing the liberation of Jerusalem from the Turks by the armies of the Catholic world in concert with those of the New World [Motolinía, 1951]. Even now, a variation of this pageant is still performed in Mexico, halfway around the world from Turkey. This globalized stereotyping was even incorporated into Webster's Dictionary under the definition of "Turk", which reads, "One exhibiting any quality attributed to Turks, such as sensuality and brutality." Much the same with the Oxford English Dictionary [Crowley, 2005]. The reference to brutality is easy to understand since battles, such as the one that took place when the Turks seized Constantinople, are brutal. Itzkowitz and I also tried to understand the reference to sensuality.

We speculated that it had a great deal to do with the youthful and virile image of Mehmed II, whose conquest was perceived as a "rape." Constantinople, which was renamed Istanbul, is still seen by today's poets as a symbol of a fallen and/or grieving woman [Halman, 1992].

As generations passed, the fall of Constantinople evolved as the major chosen trauma of the Christian West and this influenced the evolution of the Megali Idea, which crystallized in the nineteenth century. Some four decades after its independence from the Ottoman Empire, the new Greek identity became a composite of Hellenic (ancient pre-Christian Greek) and Byzantine (Christian Greek) elements. As Paschalis Kitromilides [1990] clearly described, the nation-building process of the new Greek state gradually took on two dimensions, the first being internal—the development of the independent kingdom of Greece. The other one was external and involved the influence of the Megali Idea as a point of reference for the new Greek state involving Greeks living in the Ottoman Empire in places considered as integral parts of the historical patrimony of Hellenism.

Here I will let Kyriacos Markides, a famous Cypriot-born Greek sociologist, describe his own large group's preoccupations and their role in the "Cyprus Problem". Markides refers to the Greeks' Great Idea as:

> ... a dream shared by Greeks that someday the Byzantine Empire would be restored and all the Greek lands would once again be united in Greater Greece ... The "Great Idea" found expression in ... parts of the Greek world, such as Crete and the Ionian Islands. One could argue that the "Great Idea" had an internal logic, pressing for realization in every part of the Greek world which continued to be under foreign rule. Because the Greeks of Cyprus had considered themselves historically and culturally to be Greek, the "Great Idea" has had an intense appeal. Thus, when the church fathers called on the Cypriots to fight for union with Greece, it did not require much effort to heat up emotions ... Enosis did not originate in the church but in the minds of intellectuals in their attempt to revive Greek–Byzantine civilization. However, being the most central and powerful of institutions, the church contributed immensely to its development. The church embraced the movement and for all practical purposes became its guiding nucleus. (1977, pp. 10–11)

Kyriacos Markides' remarks about the church led me to discuss the role of religion in international affairs with Dr. Volkan.

CHAPTER THIRTEEN

On belief and the psychology of religion

P ushing eight billion, our world population yields a vast amount of religious fervor and the myriad religions tend to preach the ways of goodness. It is outside our scope to accept or rebut their assertions. Archbishop Desmond Tutu said, "Religion is like a knife. If you use it to slice bread, it is good. If you use it to cut someone's hand, it is bad" (Duke, 2006). This is perhaps a good way of evoking the duality inherent in faith in respect of good and bad. Particularly note the word "use."

To Sigmund Freud, the religious obligations a person assumes are an expression of the psychological problems that were not solved in child-hood. Early years traumas feed a need to seek a father-like protection in faith, indeed to seek the love that a father has for his child and this can con-tinue throughout life. Therefore, religion is widely seen as a shared illusion (Freud, 1927c, 1930a). Early in his career, Freud rewrote the well-known sentence, "God created man in his own image" from the Book of Genesis as "Man created God in his own image" (1901b). He equated religious prac-tices with neurotic obsession, one which is universal.

Since Freud there have been a few psychoanalysts who have dealt with the subject of religion and who have sometimes questioned Freud's asser-tions. Dr. Volkan thinks that psychoanalysts have often shied away from the subject. A coldness developed between religion and psychoanalysis, just as there is a measure of conflict between religion and science in general, and

131

some people in the field decline to disclose their opinions and theories on the subject for fear of censure and rejection by publishers.

The concepts of "transitional objects" and "transitional phenomena," put forward by Donald W. Winnicott (1953a), significantly improved on psychoanalytic theories regarding the formation of religious beliefs and feelings. He associates these things as part of "normal" development in early childhood. Dr. Volkan notes that Winnicott understands the universality of transitional objects. As an example of a transitional object, Dr. Volkan cites Linus' blanket in the Charlie Brown cartoons.

> In the first year of life every baby chooses something—a transitional object—around him, whatever there is, according to its texture, smell, and movements. Sometimes even a baby's own hair can be a transitional object. Usually, the child chooses a soft object such as a teddy bear that will be under his complete control. A transitional phenomenon is something he can't touch, such as a lullaby.
>
> The transitional object or phenomenon becomes the first object representing the "non-self" in baby's mind throughout his first year. Although this first "non-self" image corresponds to something that actually exists in the outside world, the transitional object is not entirely something "non-self" because at the same time it also replaces the child's parents (or carers) who are not perceived in the child's mind to be different individuals from him or who are perceived as under the complete control of the child. This is the reason why playing with a teddy bear or having a certain tune repeated calms the child and why he sometimes thrashes the toy (or distorts the tune) without fearing the toy or carer will take revenge when he uses it as a calming object. The transitional object or phenomenon responds to the child's need for comfort, as with his mother and, like the mother, it will not abandon the child if the child rejects it. If you take away the blanket used as a transitional object and replace it with a new one, the child won't respond to the new blanket as a transitional object. A blanket that is more of a transitional object than a real mother is under the control of the child who cuddles it, clings onto it, and squeezes it. I have come across mothers who are jealous of their babies' transitional objects.
>
> Through interaction with the blanket or teddy bear or whatever, with the often-repeated lullaby, the child starts to know the

world around him. The teddy bear or the tune is not a part of the child, therefore, the child's "external reality" beyond his inner world expresses the "non-self" that the child gradually explores, creates, and comes to need. What is "created" doesn't initially correspond to the reality as an adult understands it with his or her rational way of thinking. While a child is playing with a transitional object or phenomenon, "reality" is a mixture of reality and illusion.

According to Winnicott, a baby's experience in this respect remains with him or her throughout life as an "intense experiencing that belongs to the arts and to religion and to imaginative living and to creative scientific work" (1953, p. 16).

Dr. Volkan (2013) tells us that important figures in classical psychoanalysis started to question some of Freud's ideas in the 1960s, including those about religion. He cites an example. A member of the American Psychoanalytic Association and also a Jesuit priest, William W. Meissner (1990) wrote: "If beliefs and belief systems support psychic development and help protect mental health and contribute to leading a mature life, they are not pathological, as the imaginary game in the transitional space between mother and child is not pathological, nor is Freud's own cultural work pathological" (p. 114). Meissner reminds his readers that just as a transitional object can degenerate into a (pathological) fetish, "transitional religious experience can be distorted into less authentic, relatively fetishistic directions that tend to contaminate and distort the more profoundly meaningful aspects of the religious experience" (p. 107). To Dr. Volkan's mind, Meissner does not deal with the relationship between religion and violence, rather he pursues the goal of being a peaceful intermediary between psychoanalysis and religion. Dr. Volkan says such endeavors persist today (2013).

Embarking on a line of study into terrorism perpetrated in the name of religion, Dr. Volkan took Winnicott's ideas as a starting point and has allowed us to see the developmental and creative aspects of religion as much as its regressive, destructive, and restrictive sides. In order to illustrate the progressive and regressive functions of transitional objects and phenomena, Dr. Volkan (2013) uses the metaphor of a lantern with one opaque and one transparent side placed between the infant and his environment.

When infants feel comfortable, fed, rested, and loved they turn the lantern's transparent, bright side towards their surroundings, they illuminate the objects around them, and they slowly begin to perceive these objects as entities separate from themselves. Dr. Volkan holds that the infant needs exercises in which illusion and reality are mixed before the child develops better perceptions and ideas about the real world. When infants feel uncomfortable, hungry, or sleepy they turn the opaque side of the lantern towards the frustrating outside world. This "wipes out" surrounding reality. Most mothers have observed that when their toddlers are falling asleep, they hold onto their blankets as if their whole world consists of themselves and the blanket. At such times, the transitional object serves as a mother substitute protecting the child from the rest of the world. Dr. Volkan also stresses that when the metaphorical lantern is thus turned opaque side out, we can imagine that the child's mind experiences a sense of omnipotence in its little sphere. This happens many times as the child alternates between getting to know reality on the outside and retreating to the lonely, narcissistic little world of one's own. Eventually, the child begins to hold onto unalterable external realities such as the mother being a separate being, sometimes comforting, sometimes frustrating. Colors become discernible, items nearby are seen as distinct objects, and gradually the "game" illustrated by the image of the lantern tilts in favor of the bright side which illuminates the outside world.

Vamık Volkan:

> By using teddy bears, blankets, or other transitional objects and phenomena, toddlers reach an important milestone. If a child's development is normal, she eventually accepts the "non-self" world, even the indifference of the universe, adjusts to a rational mentality, and sets aside transitional objects and phenomena. However, the function of transitional objects and phenomena remains a part of our psychic life and they emerge in adulthood in what we can call rationality's "resting moments." At such times a differentiation between reality and illusion is suspended.

Vamık Volkan has a first-hand experience of this to relate:

> On my first visit to Jerusalem in 1980, my friend Avner Falk took me to the Old City. Instead of walking around the streets, he took me to the rooftops of houses overlooking the old historical city. This experience led me to have one of the most memorable "resting moments" of my life. It was an indescribable feeling. I can now explain rationally how irrational it was. I felt as if the entire history of humanity

over hundreds of generations was flowing through my body and that I now comprehended what it meant to be a human being. Moments of this nature show how we relate to transitional objects and other phenomena, things which echo down our entire lives.

The need for "resting moments" and the duration of these moments varies from person to person and from group to group. At such a moment, a Christian may well know that a woman cannot become pregnant in the absence of sperm yet simultaneously believes in the virgin birth. The rational view of angels is that nobody has ever seen one, yet rational people often behave as if they exist. Some people might say they don't need religious "resting moments," but they might well be calling the same thing by another name. For instance, they might play games related to astrology or draw pictures revealing a mixture of illusion and reality.

The biggest and the best arranged socially approved propaganda in relation to children is performed by those religious organizations of which parents, teachers, and neighbors are members. Children not only identify with their parents' religious beliefs, they are also exposed to outside religious propaganda as they grow up. As a mixture of reality and illusion, religion crystallizes as a "psychic reality" in people's minds. It allows for experiencing "resting moments" regularly and it often affects large-group identity—or subgroup identity—by merging with nationalism and the sense of ethnicity. As with the "normal" boundaries of psychological health, the "normal" boundaries of religious beliefs and acts are usually socially determined.

I would say that religious beliefs and feelings derive from the normal development processes in early childhood and from the times when we need "resting moments" in adulthood.

Dr. Volkan contends, therefore, that people's investment in religion comes not only from childhood fears and traumas and the child's needs in relation to the father, as Freud writes, but that it is more spectral than that. The individual psychology of the developing human, sociocultural experiences, education, and the level of exposure to religious themes are also at play.

Dr. Volkan uses the term "proto-symbol" (Volkan, 1995; Werner & Kaplan, 1963) to shed light on religious experience. People know perfectly well that a symbol is used in place of another object, but perceptions can become blurred. Under certain circumstances the symbol can be perceived to actually be what it represents and then it becomes, in Dr. Volkan's opinion, a proto-symbol. A depiction of Jesus Christ in a church is a symbolic representation, yet its beholders will often feel that they are in the presence of Christ. With transubstantiation, one knows the wafer and wine proffered at the altar are symbols; but the Church contends that they actually *are* the body and blood of Christ and millions go along with this.

Dr. Volkan (2013) discusses this subject in depth in his book *Enemies on the Couch: A Psychopolitical Journey through War and Peace.* He writes that as individuals go through their cycles of life, they may use religion to fulfill or meet their various needs and desires and address their internal tensions and conflicts. He concedes that the emotional connection Freud made between God and the father image is indeed true for some people. However, he says, the God image represents for each individual an amalgam of parental love, fear of punishment, a feeling of or wish for omnipotence, and most importantly, the sense of belonging to a family, a clan, or a large group.

Returning to the lantern metaphor, Dr. Volkan suggests fundamentalists always turn the opaque side of the lantern to the outside world, as it were. When they hold onto transitional objects (to give an example, again from his work) while going to sleep, unlike babies who are cocooned from the outside world, adult fundamentalists are all too aware of the actual environment that they perceive to be threatening them. Therefore, the "resting moment" of such individuals is not a peaceful moment. People who turn the opaque side of their lanterns to the real world often seek a leader and protector whom they hope will meet their needs. Yet Dr. Volkan holds that religious fundamentalist leaders deliberately turn the opaque sides of their lanterns to the outside world in order to exaggerate its dangers. After all, the enemy we cannot see is much more dangerous than the one we can. A tense attitude towards the outside world is maintained. And often enough, in the ultimate act of aggression against both oneself and others, a fundamentalist will kill himself to escape the dangers of this world and to join God in the next. He or she may well take their fellow men, women, children, and babies with them to the hereafter.

J. Anderson Thomson, former assistant director of the Center for the Study of Mind and Human Interaction (CSMHI), asks a simple question— why do we believe in God? To answer it he draws on rather less simple things, such as psychoanalysis, cognitive hypotheses, and evolutionary psychology. The conclusion Thomson comes to is that "Religion may offer comfort in a harsh world; it may foster community; it may incite conflict. In short, it may have its uses—for good and for evil" (2011, p. 116). Yet to Thomson, "Religion was created by human beings and this would be a better world if we ceased confusing it with fact" (p. 116). Thomson also says, "Despite the political correctness of proclaiming that there is no conflict between science and religion, the constant din of battle in school boards and educational committees in the United States, Canada and United Kingdom is becoming deafening" (p. 116). Essentially, Thomson comes to the conclusion that war is raging between religion and science.

Dr. Volkan has no doubt that religion will continue to play a role in people's lives. He thinks as regressions occur in large groups, more members of these groups will hold onto religion and that social scientists all over the world should be braver and feel freer to research into the reasons why religion is at times used as a knife to cut someone's hand (Suistola & Volkan, 2017).

CHAPTER FOURTEEN

A psychopolitical approach for the reduction of large-group conflict: the Tree Model

With Estonian children in Tartu, Estonia, 1996.

Whenlarge groups are in con-flict, most of their political, legal, economic, military, and other "real-world" concerns are also contaminated with psychological issues. Those who are assigned to deal with these conflicts on an official level establish short- and long-term strate-gies, "rules of the game," and mobilize resources to implement their ideas. In so doing they may seek a psycho-logical advantage over the "enemy" using elements of "surface psychol-ogy" such as conscious assumptions for gaining the upper hand in matters

With the future Estonian president Arnold Rüütel, 1996.

of ethnic, national, or ideological interest. There is, however, another type of psychology that triggers more hidden, mostly unconscious, resistances that thwart peaceful, adaptive solutions to national and ethnic conflicts. Dr. Volkan believes that in certain protracted conflicts understanding this second type of psychology is essential in finding more creative solutions for the reduction of tensions between enemies. At the core of this psychology lie the concepts of large-group identity and large-group rituals which, when understood, can help elucidate some of the seemingly irrational aspects of conflicts. The method to be described here involves a "neutral" third party team that seeks to help the opposing parties have more realistic discussions and develop more adaptive strategies for dealing with their conflict.

The Center for the Study of Mind and Human Interaction (CSMHI) has developed a methodology, called the "Tree Model," based on Dr. Volkan's understanding of what constitutes a large-group identity and the ritu-als that are performed to protect, maintain, or repair this shared identity. The approach maintains that an interdisciplinary third-party facilitating team—composed of psychoanalysts and other clinicians specializing in international relations, along with diplomats, historians, and other social scientists—can help opposing parties to decrease or remove the psycho-logical poisons between them so that they can engage in more realistic negotiations. This method is in some ways quite different from the "con-flict resolution" activities practiced by many nongovernmental organization

(NGO) programs that have sprung up during recent decades. Most NGO conflict resolution efforts attempt to erase the psychological wall that has become rigidified between enemy groups. CSMHI's method, however, maintains this wall in order to decrease anxiety over large-group identity issues. It allows the opposing groups—without giving them advice—to transform their antagonistic rituals into more peaceful rituals and makes the wall separating them more flexible and permeable.

The Tree Model is a multi-year process with three components: 1) psychopolitical assessments (roots of the tree); 2) psychopolitical dialogues (the trunk of the tree); 3) institution building (branches of the tree).

Psychopolitical assessments (roots of the tree)

The first step in any effort at unofficial diplomacy should involve an assessment or diagnosis of the problems to be addressed. CSMHI believe that large-group problems can only be fully diagnosed on location. Before traveling to a particular country or region to begin work, CSMHI's interdisciplinary team study the history and culture of the antagonist groups, collect information on the current situation, and identify problems. From the beginning, it is clear that interdisciplinary collaboration is needed. Even though the historian on the team may not be an expert in the particular country, he brings a methodology and a way of thinking that contributes to understanding the information gathered. Clinicians bring understanding of the mental representation of historical events and how they may be shared by members of a large group. Regional experts are consulted, as are the local newspapers when available, and other sources. At the end of this preparatory time, the team draws up a list of problems, local contacts, and potential partners who may be able to provide further contacts and information.

Every conflict has its "hot" locations. These may include national cemeteries, memorials to those who have died in large-group conflicts, and other historically important or symbolic locales. Visiting such places with members of the groups in conflict allows the facilitating team to get quickly to the heart of what these sites represent and why they are perceived as hot in the context of the conflict. During this assessment phase, Dr. Volkan and his team examine how elements of a large group's identity are heightened when the group is threatened and under stress. This preoccupation colors every aspect of the conflict and the relationship with the opposing group.

Vamık Volkan:

> For example, Estonians were naturally euphoric after regaining
> their independence from the Soviet Union in 1991. But CSMHI was
> able to uncover other less obvious aspects of the Estonian outlook
> through intensive interviews with a wide range of Estonians and
> through visits to "hot" places such as the former Soviet nuclear
> submarine base at Paldiski. What my team members and I found was
> that Estonians suffered from an underlying anxiety of "disappearing"
> as an ethnic group, of ceasing to exist. With the exception of a brief
> period of independence between 1918–1940, Estonians have lived
> for a millennium under the domination of others. When at last they
> had regained their independence in 1991, they remained anxious
> that they would once again be swallowed up by a neighboring group
> (Russians, in this case). Estonians' anxiety over foreign domination
> was also fueled by the fact that every third resident of Estonia was
> ethnic Russian or a Russian-speaker.

While there were plenty of real-world issues to attend to, the perception that
Estonia would "disappear" caused resistance to policies for integrating the
"non-Estonian" people living in Estonia. If Estonian and Russian "blood"
were to "mix," the uniqueness of the Estonian people—whose sense of identity had managed to persist despite their small numbers and adverse conditions over the centuries—might not survive. Dr. Volkan's and his team's
diagnosis then indicated the need to help Estonians differentiate real issues
from fantasized fears so that they could deal more adaptively with the integration of Russian-speakers living in Estonia.

Psychopolitical dialogues (the trunk of the tree)

After diagnosis, the next step is to convene a series of psychopolitical dialogues among members of the opposing groups or within a single group if
there is internal fragmentation. Ten to fifteen participants from each side are
selected, ideally influential officials and policy makers, meeting in a strictly
unofficial capacity. These selected participants meet with Dr. Volkan and his
team for four days at a time, several times a year, as these discussion groups
become a "laboratory" for what goes on in the large groups they represent.
In this laboratory, the facilitators can see and help identify the rituals that are

activated to protect the large-group identities. Some of these rituals are malig-
nant and impede rational progress toward peace, recovery, and coexistence.

For example, during the first day of an initial meeting between influential
Turks and Greeks discussing their conflicts over the Aegean Sea and Cyprus,
frustrated emotions were high as participants expressed their perceptions
of the "enemy." That evening at dinner, participants enjoyed each other as
"friends." During the next morning's meeting, a Greek participant spoke of
her confusion: She had felt hurt and angry during the day and friendly at the
dinner. How was she supposed to behave? The facilitators then helped her
see how her personal identity and large-group identity are on a continuum
and that, during the meeting, she had inevitably become a spokesperson
of her large group, while at dinner, her individual identity held sway. She
and the other Greek and Turkish participants were asked to let themselves
wear the canvas of their large-group identity as their garment during the
meetings. This would be the only way to observe the psychodynamics of
Turkish–Greek interactions at close range. In other words, CSMHI did not
try to force an emotionally civil atmosphere at the meetings, but rather
aimed to allow emotions, including anxiety and anger, to be expressed at an
appropriate level. The clinicians on the CSMHI team try to ensure that such
emotions remain useful for insights into the conflict, and that the emotions
neither degenerate to destructive levels nor are so denied that only detached
intellectual statements are made during meetings.

Vamık Volkan:

> The psychopolitical dialogues were central to the success of the
> Tree Model. The facilitating team was interdisciplinary, including
> diplomats, historians, and other social scientists, as well as psycho-
> analysts and psychiatrists. The clinicians were crucial to the process
> as they draw upon their years of experience in the clinical setting
> to conduct such meetings. Their expertise included the ability to
> "hear" multiple meanings behind the statements made by partici-
> pants, to tolerate affects, to help participants understand their large-
> group perceptions and rituals, and to serve as models for empathic
> understanding of the "enemy."

There were certain key patterns of behavior, concepts, and strategies that
characterized the process of psychopolitical dialogues. They evolved and
repeated during each four-day meeting as well as in a larger process over

the entire two- to three-year series. The following are brief descriptions of various behavior patterns that CSMHI have observed during psychopolitical dialogues between Estonians and Russians, Arabs and Israelis, Turks and Greeks, South Ossetians and Georgians, and Croats, Serbs, and Bosniaks.

Displacement onto a mini-conflict

Sometimes, at the outset of a dialogue meeting, a disruptive situation evolves abruptly and absorbs the attention and energy of all participants. Such a situation is usually marked with a sense of urgency, yet the content of this "crisis" is essentially insignificant in comparison to the salient aspects of the ethnic or national conflict for which the dialogue meeting has been organized. It is reminiscent of the extended debates on who sits where at a conference table that sometimes occur prior to important negotiations between nations. Dr. Volkan calls these "mini-conflicts," and while seemingly inexplicable and incongruous—much like the masques that precede an Elizabethan tragedy—they provide condensed and symbolically suggestive treatments of what will be explored dramatically later in the play itself.

The echo phenomenon

When representatives of opposing sides open a discussion, the echo of recent events involving their large groups can often be heard in their exchanges, further igniting emotions that exacerbate resistances to adaptive discussions. During psychopolitical dialogues, Dr. Volkan has seen the shadow of some recent military or political development fall over the work group. It then becomes necessary to acknowledge and assimilate this shadow and its meaning for both sides before realistic negotiation can continue.

Competition to express chosen traumas and chosen glories

Members of opposing groups in dialogue frequently enter into a competition to list historical grievances (*chosen traumas*) and past triumphs (*chosen glories*). In addition to ancestral traumas and glories, other more recent derivatives of these events are also chronicled. Chosen traumas are more effective than chosen glories in promoting group cohesion. Consequently, listings of chosen traumas during a dialogue tend to be more prominent than references to ancestors' successes.

Vamık Volkan:

> At unofficial dialogue meetings, the competition to list grievances, especially at the outset, seems involuntary and occurs according to the principle of "the egoism of victimization" [Mack, 1979]: there is no empathy for the other side's losses and injuries. The task of the facilitating team, therefore, is to serve as models for empathic listening.

The accordion phenomenon

After some airing of chosen traumas and chosen glories, or their derivatives, and when more empathic communication begins, the opposing groups often experience a rapprochement. This closeness is then followed by a sudden withdrawal from one another and then again by closeness. The pattern repeats numerous times.

Vamık Volkan:

> I liken this to the playing of an accordion—squeezing together and then pulling apart. Initial distancing is a defensive maneuver to keep aggressive attitudes and feelings in check, since, if the opponents were to come together, they might harm one another—at least in fantasy—or in turn become targets of retaliation. When opposing teams are confined together in one room, sharing conscious efforts for peace, sometimes they must deny their aggressive feelings as they press together in a kind of illusory union. When this becomes oppressive, it feels dangerous, and distancing occurs again. The most realistic discussions take place after the facilitating team has allowed the accordion to play for a while, until the squeezing and distancing become less extreme.

Projections and projective identification

Members of one group in conflict may attempt to define their identity through externalizing unwanted parts of themselves onto the enemy, projecting their unwanted thoughts, perceptions, and wishes. For example, it is not *"we"* who are troublemakers, but *"them"*. Often projections onto the opposing group reflect a clear "us" and "them" dichotomy of rigid positions: we are "good," they are "bad."

Vamık Volkan:

> During a dialogue series, projections can also involve a more complex relationship between representatives of the two opposing large groups in a pattern similar to the mechanism of "projective identification" [Klein, 1946] that psychoanalysts see in individual patients. At the group level, one team may project onto the other their own wishes for how the opposing side should think, feel, or behave. The first team then identifies with the other that houses their projections—this other is perceived as actually acting in accordance with the expectations of the former. In effect, one team becomes the "spokesperson" for the other team, and since this process takes place unconsciously, the first team actually believes their remarks about the enemy. However, the resulting "relationship" is not real since it is based on the processes of only one party. The facilitating team interprets or interferes with the development of projective identification, since once it develops, the reality of perceptions is compromised.

Personal stories

Participants in dialogues invariably bring up personal stories pertaining to the large-group conflict at hand. Initially, personal stories often reflect an "us" and "them" (or "me" and "them") psychology in a black and white manner—the other is seen as "bad" while one's own group is experienced as "good."
    Vamık Volkan:

> This is similar to the mechanism of splitting that clinicians see among certain patients who divide and experience themselves, intimate others, and their mental images as either all "good" or all "bad." As empathy evolves, however, stories begin to include ambivalences. To have ambivalence is to begin to acknowledge the other's identity as a total being who is both similar and dissimilar, liked and disliked; the other begins to become more human.

Minor differences

When parties become genuinely more empathic toward each other, they may become anxious if they begin to perceive themselves and their group as too similar to the enemy. As each side's projection of unwanted aspects becomes unstable due to the perception that the other is similar to one's own group, participants may exaggerate the importance of minor differences between them to maintain their separate identities.

Vamık Volkan:

> Minor differences thus function as a border separating the opposing parties so that their respective identities remain intact. A seemingly trivial disparity may then take on monumental importance and turn positive discussions sour. We have found that minor differences between opposing groups are often psychologically harder to deal with than major differences, such as language or religion. When minor differences become resistances, the facilitating team tries to enhance and verify each group's identity, so that the minor differences remain minor.

Symbolizing the conflict and "playing" with it

A symbol or metaphor that represents important aspects of the conflict may emerge from within the dialogue. For example, the weaker party may call itself a mouse while referring to the stronger enemy as an elephant. Eventually, the participants begin to "play" with this metaphor, to kick it around like a ball (Volkan, 2011).

Vamık Volkan:

> As the meeting series progresses, the metaphor captures the attention of the participants and transforms diffuse emotions and blurred realities into a more concrete understanding of the problem. The playful metaphor connects the participants, allowing them to share in the game, while at the same time addressing a critical issue. As this play continues, poisonous emotions begin to disappear, and laughter often accompanies the banter. Realistic discussion of issues can then ensue.
>
> It is important to note that the facilitating team should not introduce or fabricate a metaphor or "toy" for the participants to play with—it must be created or provided by the participants themselves. One positive side-effect of the participants' creating and playing with symbols and metaphors during the dialogue series is the transformation of large-group proto-symbols (things that

become what they represent) into symbols. In warlike situations, large groups' cultural amplifiers are perceived by one or both sides as proto-symbols, not merely symbols but real. To turn them back into symbols is a sign of progress.

Time expansion

As noted earlier, when chosen traumas and their derivatives are reactivated, the emotions and perceptions pertaining to them are felt as if the trauma occurred recently—they become fused with emotions and perceptions pertaining to the present and are even projected into the future. Understandably, this time collapse complicates attempts to resolve the conflicts at hand. To counteract this phenomenon and to encourage a time expansion, facilitators must allow discussions to take place concerning the chosen trauma itself and participants' personal traumas pertaining to the large-group conflict. If feelings and issues about the past can be distanced and separated from present problems, then today's problems can be more realistically discussed.

Mourning

Opposing parties come to unofficial diplomacy meetings with aspirations, hopes, and opinions that tend to be rigid and unrealistic. A successful dialogue seeks to tame and loosen such positions, but this is difficult if the losses that result from an altered position or status are not mourned.

Vamık Volkan:

> From a clinical point of view, human beings must mourn when they give up something or when they lose a stubbornly held position. Mourning in this sense does not refer to observable behavior such as crying, but to psychodynamic processes that occur after loss. The neutral facilitators must be sensitive to the mourning process and to the liberation and acceptance of change that it provides.

Institution building (branches of the tree)

Based on observation and understanding of the above processes as they take place during the dialogues, the facilitating team intervenes and guides the discussions to weaken or remove the psychological obstacles and to enable the participants to communicate more realistically with each other. In time, they begin to develop creative ideas for applying and promoting these new ways of thinking and interacting.

This third component of the Tree Model involves transferring the insights from the dialogues into concrete actions affecting the societies involved.

Vamık Volkan:

> In collaboration with the dialogue participants and local contacts trained in the CSMHI methodology, the CSMHI team sought to prevent stagnation or slipping backwards by institutionalizing the progress that has been made. The local contact groups included clinicians trained to work in the societies involved at the grass roots level to create models for coexistence or collaboration.
>
> In Estonia, for example, within three years following the psychopolitical dialogues between Estonians and Russians, we were able to build model coexistence projects in two villages where the population is half Estonian and half Russian. We also created a model to promote integration among Estonian and Russian schoolchildren and influenced the language examination required for Russians to become Estonian citizens. The most important task here was to "teach" people at the grass roots level to gain political power, and to help local contact groups to evolve as effective NGOs.

There are, of course, limitations to this model. First, it requires that psychoanalysts and other clinicians develop expertise in international relations and collaborate with diplomats, political scientists, and historians. Building an interdisciplinary team has its own psychodynamic challenges. Second, the tree needs water (funds) and it can be difficult to find sponsors for a process that will take some years before the fruits of the tree can be observed by everyone. Nevertheless, the Tree Model is offered as a methodology for a new type of preventive or corrective diplomacy carried out systematically by a neutral third party.

As far as I am concerned, the Tree Model is the only psychoanalytically informed, interdisciplinary methodology for finding peaceful coexistence between enemy groups. It is beyond the scope of this book to describe this methodology further, but its most detailed description can be found in Dr. Volkan's books, *Killing in the Name of Identity* (2006) and *Enemies on The Couch* (2013).

Last words

Vamık Volkan's 80th birthday party, House of Lords, London, 2012. Hosted by Lord John Alderdice (middle), guests included Robert Friedman from Israel (left).

In 2004, Vamık Volkan received a letter from John Lineweaver, a peace activist from Long Island, New York. The letter informed him that he was being considered for a nomination for the Nobel Peace Prize for his work on conflicts between opposing large groups and for his thirty or so years carrying out projects in various trouble spots around the world and for developing psychopolitical theories. John Lineweaver had been in Charlottesville several times attending academic programs which were open to the public at the Center for the Study of Mind and Human Interaction (CSMHI). He had been involved with various societies and NGOs associated with the UN, so he was not unknown to Vamık. Dr. Volkan wondered whether he should thank John Lineweaver for thinking of him and leave it at that.

At the Carter Center's International Negotiation Network (INN), Vamık Volkan had met several Nobel laureates without considering how he might join them. Friends opined that talk of a possible nomination could attract attention to psychological aspects of international relations. John Lineweaver pressed on and in a short space of time letters reached the Nobel committee from twenty-seven countries in support of Dr. Volkan's nomination.

Vamık Volkan:

> I had met several Nobel Peace Prize laureates, but I had never put myself in this category. When John Lineweaver showed me the letters of support, I was most grateful for the honors heaped upon me by many distinguished people from many parts of the world. In fact, I was moved. While I was a Fulbright Scholar in Vienna in 2006, when introducing me at meetings or social gatherings, persons from the Sigmund Freud Foundation would often make reference to my candidacy for the Nobel Peace Prize. But it was only after my three-month stay in Istanbul in 2007 as a visiting professor at Bahçeşehir University and Cerrahpaşa Medical School that the name Nobel was pinned on my lapel, as it were. I was quite chuffed about it, of course, but also rather embarrassed. Reporters sought me out to discover what was going on in Turkey and the wider world and I became a guest on talk shows. For decades, I had carried out my academic and psychopolitical activities well under the radar of the popular media, but no longer. My reason for allowing myself to be in the spotlight now was my urge to share my ideas concerning

major identity crises in Turkey and also to express my opinion on women's rights.

Five nominations and many years later, the prize has eluded Dr. Volkan.

While this book was being written, Vamık Volkan received the Mary Sigourney Award, the most prestigious award in the field of psychoanalysis. In a ceremony at the Waldorf Astoria Hotel in New York on January 15, 2015 the award was presented—just two days before a gala dinner, also in NYC, to celebrate the diamond jubilee of the *American Journal of Psychoanalysis* of which Vamık Volkan was the guest editor.

The Mary Sigourney Award was conferred on two people in that year. One of the awards was given to psychologist Jay Greenberg for his editorship of journals in the field of psychoanalysis and for facilitating their dissemination and strategic cooperation with like journals around the world.

The other was given to Dr. Volkan for two reasons. One was for being a "seminal contributor to the application of psychoanalytic thinking to conflicts between countries and cultures," and the other was the fact that his "clinical thinking about the use of object relations theory in primitive mental states has advanced understanding of severe personality disorders."

Since 1979, Dr. Volkan, as a psychiatrist and psychoanalyst, has tried to understand world affairs. At this time, the psychoanalytic establishment in America was of the opinion that such matters were of no concern in their profession. Opinions modified over the years and by the time Dr. Volkan received the Mary Sigourney Award this, unlike his Nobel nomination, came as no surprise. His "new horizon" had been officially accepted.

It has been no easy task to capture the life and works of this prolific man and I am well aware that this book is far from comprehensive. At the time of writing, Vamık is still producing new work. Vamık and I have exchanged signed copies of our various books down the years with great pleasure. He wrote, "*You have helped me get to know myself better thanks to this book*" on one of my works, which has been a source of great pride and always will be. That he wrote on one of them is a prize for me that I will carry with pride for the rest of my life. My idea on the name of this book formed after his sentence above that moved me and I gave it the name it has.

As we go to print, Vamık is ensconced in his home in Ozanköy, Kyrenia for the summer months surrounded by his family. He remains upbeat about the positive effects of the psychoanalytical contributions to healing global wounds and inhibiting repetitions. He continues his prolific output of books and I hope that this one will meet with his approval and yours.

For the steep learning curve, I thank Dr. Volkan with all my heart. I also thank his wife Elizabeth, who is a great part of Vamık Volkan's life force.

Vamık dropped a couple of words once when discussing his experiences in conflict zones, the pain he shared with those concerned, the fear he read in children's eyes, the hope of a far brighter future: "*Understand humanity.*"

References

Afetinan, A. (1971). *M. Kemal Atatürk'ten Yazdıklarım (My Memories of M. Kemal Atatürk)*. Istanbul: Turkish Ministry of Education Publishing House.

Akhtar, S. (1984). The syndrome of identity diffusion. *American Journal of Psychiatry, 141*: 1381–1385.

Akhtar, S. (2010). *Immigration and Acculturation: Mourning, Adaptation, and the Next Generation*. New York: Jason Aronson.

Angelou, M. (1970). *I Know Why the Caged Bird Sings*. New York: Random House.

Atatürk, M. K. (1952). *Atatürk'ün Söylev ve Demeçleri (Speeches and Statements by Atatürk)*. 2 vols. Istanbul: Türk Inkilap Tarihi Enstitüsü.

Aydemir, Ş. S. (1969). *Tek Adam (The Only Man)*, vol. 1. Istanbul: Remzi.

Barrie, J. M. (1906). *Peter Pan in Kensington Gardens*. London: Hodder & Stoughton.

Bergmann, M. S. (1973). Limitations of method in psychoanalytic biography: A historical inquiry. *Journal of the American Psychoanalytic Association, 21*: 833–850.

Berkes, N. (1975). *Türk Düşününde Batı Sorunu (The Western Question in Turkish Thought)*. Ankara, Turkey: Bilgi.

Bloom, P. (2010). *How Pleasure Works: The New Science of Why We Like What We Like*. New York: W. W. Norton.

Blos, P. (1979). *The Adolescence Passage*. New York: International Universities Press.

Boyer, L. B. (1986). One man's need to have enemies: A psychoanalytic perspective. *Journal of Psychoanalytic Anthropology, 9*: 101–120.

Brazelton, T. B., & Greenspan, S. I. (2000). *The Irreducible Needs of Children: What Every Child Must Have to Grow, Learn and Flourish*. Cambridge, MA: Perseus.

Crowley, R. (2005). *Constantinople, the Last Great Siege, 1453*. London: Faber & Faber.

Darwin, C. (1859). *On the Origin of Species by Means of Natural Selection, or the Preservation of Favoured Races in the Struggle for Life*. London: John Murray.

Davies, N. (1996). *Europe, a History*. London: Pimlico.

Dixon, N. (1976). *On the Psychology of Military Incompetence*. London: Jonathan Cape.

Duke, L. (2006, September 9). Archbishop Desmond Tutu looks back, definitely not in anger. *Washington Post*, pp. V1–V8.

Emde, R. (1991). Positive emotions for psychoanalytic theory: Surprises from infancy research and new directions. *Journal of the American Psychoanalytic Association* (Supplement), *39*: 5–44.

Emin, A. (Yalman). (1922, January 10). Büyük Millet Meclisi Reisi Başkumandan Mustafa Kemal Paşa ile bir mülâkat (An interview with Mustafa Kemal Pasha, president of the Grand National Assembly and commander-in-chief). *Vakit* (a Turkish daily).

Erikson, E. H. (1956). The problem of ego identity. *Journal of the American Psychoanalytic Association*, *4*: 56–121.

Erikson, E. H. (1958). *Young Man Luther*. New York: W. W. Norton.

Erikson, E. H. (1985). *Childhood and Society*. New York: W. W. Norton.

Ersoy, M. A. (1998). Chosen traumas of the Alavis in Anatolia. *Mind and Human Interaction*, *9*: 38–51.

Freud, S. (1901b). The forgetting of names and sets of words. In: *The Psychopathology of Everyday Life. S. E.*, *6*: 273–301. London: Hogarth.

Freud, S. (1910c). *Leonardo da Vinci and a Memory of His Childhood. S. E.*, *11*: 57–137. London: Hogarth.

Freud, S. (1917e). Mourning and melancholia. *S. E.*, *14*: 237–258. London: Hogarth.

Freud, S, (1927c). *The Future of an Illusion. S. E.*, *21*: 5–56. London: Hogarth.

Freud, S. (1930a). *Civilization and Its Discontents. S. E.*, *21*: 197–215. London: Hogarth.

Freud, S. (1937b). Moses an Egyptian. In: *Moses and Monotheism* (1939a). *S. E.*, *23*: 1–137. London: Hogarth.

Freud, S. (1941e). Address to the Members of the B'nai B'rith. *S. E.*, *20*: 271–274. London: Hogarth.

Goodall, J. (2010). *Through a Window: My Thirty Years with the Chimpanzees of Gombe*. New York: Houghton Mifflin Harcourt.

Greenspan, S. I. (1981). *Psychopathology and Adaptation in Infancy and Early Childhood.* New York: International Universities Press.

Halman, T. H. (1992). Istanbul. In: *The Last Lullaby* (pp. 8–9). Merrick, NY: Cross Cultural Communications.

Julius, D. A. (1992). Biculturalism and international independence. *Mind and Human Interaction, 3:* 53–56.

Kernberg, O. F. (1975). *Borderline Conditions and Pathological Narcissism.* New York: Jason Aronson.

Kernberg, O. F. (1980). *Internal World and External Reality: Object Relations Theory Applied.* New York: Jason Aronson.

Kinross, Lord (1965). *Atatürk: A Biography of Mustafa Kemal, Father of Modern Turkey.* New York: William Morrow.

Kitromilides, P. M. (1990). Imagined communities and the origins of the national question in the Balkans. In: M. Blickhorn & T. Veremis (Eds.), *Modern Greek Nationalism and Nationality* (pp. 23–65). Athens: Sage-Eliamep.

Klein, M. (1946). Notes on some schizoid mechanisms. *International Journal of Psychoanalysis, 27:* 99–110.

Kohut, H. (1971). *The Analysis of the Self: A Systematic Approach to the Treatment of Narcissistic Personality Disorders.* New York: International Universities Press.

Kris, E. (1975). *Selected Papers of Ernst Kris.* New Haven, CT: Yale University Press.

Lee, H. (1961). *To Kill a Mockingbird.* New York: Harper & Row.

Lehtonen, J. (2003). The dream between neuroscience and psychoanalysis: Has feeding an infant impact on brain function and the capacity to create dream images in infants? *Psychoanalysis in Europe, 57:* 175–182.

Lehtonen, J. (2016). Self before self: On the scenic model of the early embodied self. *Journal of Consciousness Studies, 23:* 214–236.

Lewis, B. (1968). *The Emergence of Modern Turkey.* London: Oxford University Press.

Loewenberg, P. (1994). The psychological reality of nationalism: Between community and fantasy. *Mind and Human Interaction, 5:* 6–18.

Loewenberg, P. (1995). *Fantasy and Reality in History.* London: Oxford University Press.

Mack, J. (1979). Foreword. In: V. D. Volkan, *Cyprus: War and Adaptation* (pp. ix–xxi). Charlottesville, VA: University of Virginia Press.

Mango, A. (2002). *Atatürk: The Biography of the Founder of Modern Turkey.* New York: Overlook Press.

Markides, K. C. (1977). *The Rise and Fall of the Cyprus Republic.* New Haven, CT: Yale University Press.

Mavratsas, C. (1997). The ideological context between Greek-Cypriot nationalism and Cypriotism 1974–1995: Politics, social memory and identity. *Ethnic and Racial Studies, 20*: 715–725.

Meissner, W. W. (1990). The role of transitional conceptualization in religious thought. In: J. H. Smith & S. A. Handelman (Eds.), *Psychoanalysis and Religion* (pp. 95–116). Baltimore, MD: Johns Hopkins University Press.

Motolinía, T. de (1951). *History of Indians of New Spain.* F. B. Steck (Trans.). Washington, DC: Academy of American Franciscan History.

Murphy, R. F. (1957). Ingroup hostility and social cohesion. *American Anthropologist, 59*: 1018–1035.

Ortaylı, I. (2007). On the history of Cyprus. Keynote speech, the Sixth International Congress on Cyprus Studies, Eastern Mediterranean University, Gazi Mağusa, TRNC, October 24.

Purhonen, M., Kilpeläinen-Lees, R., Valkonen-Korhonen, M., Karhu, J., & Lehtonen, J. (2005). Four-month-old infants process own mother's voice faster than unfamiliar voices – electrical signs of sensitization in infant brain. *Cognitive Brain Research, 3*: 627–633.

Schwoebel, R. (1967). *The Shadows of Crescent: The Renaissance Image of Turks (1453–1717).* New York: St. Martin's Press.

Simmons, M. (2015). *The British and Cyprus.* Stroud, UK: The History Press.

Stein, H. F. (1990). The international and group milieu of ethnicity: Identifying generic group dynamic issues. *Canadian Review of Studies in Nationalism, 17*: 107–130.

Stein, H. F. (1993). The Slovak- and Rusyn-American experience: Ethnic adaptation in the Steel Valley of western Pennsylvania. *Mind and Human Interaction, 4*: 83–91.

Stern, D. N. (1985). *The Interpersonal World of the Infant.* New York: Basic Books.

Suistola, J., & Volkan, V. D. (2017). *Religious Knives: Historical and Psychological Dimensions of International Terrorism.* Durham, NC: Pitchstone.

Thomson, J. A. (with Aukofer, C.) (2011). *Why We Believe in God(s): A Concise Guide to the Science of Faith.* Charlottesville, VA: Pitchstone.

Thomson, J. A., Harris, M., Volkan, V. D., & Edwards, B. (1995). The psychology of Western European neo-racism. *International Journal of Group Rights, 3*: 1–30.

Varnava, A., & Faustmann, H. (Eds.) (2009). *Reunifying Cyprus: The Annan Plan and Beyond.* Library of Modern Middle East Studies. London: I. B. Tauris.

Volkan, V. D. (1972). The "linking objects" of pathological mourners. *Archives of General Psychiatry, 27*: 215–222.

Volkan, V. D. (1973). Transitional fantasies in the analysis of a narcissistic personality. *Journal of the American Psychoanalytic Association, 21*: 351–376.

Volkan, V. D. (1976). *Primitive Internalized Object Relations: A Clinical Study of Schizophrenic, Borderline and Narcissistic Patients.* New York: International Universities Press.

Volkan, V. D. (1979). *Cyprus: War and Adaptation. The Psychoanalytic History of Two Ethnic Groups in Conflict.* Charlottesville, VA: University of Virginia Press.

Volkan, V. D. (1981). *Linking Objects and Linking Phenomena: A Study of the Forms, Symptoms, Metapsychology and Therapy of Complicated Mourning.* New York: International Universities Press.

Volkan, V. D. (1988). *The Need to Have Enemies and Allies: From Clinical Practice to International Relationships.* Northvale, NJ: Jason Aronson.

Volkan, V. D. (1991). On chosen trauma. *Mind and Human Interaction, 4*: 3–19.

Volkan, V. D. (1995). *The Infantile Psychotic Self: Understanding and Treating Schizophrenics and Other Difficult Patients.* Northvale, NJ: Jason Aronson.

Volkan, V. D. (1996). Bosnia-Herzegovina: Ancient fuel of a modern inferno. *Mind and Human Interaction, 7*: 110–127.

Volkan, V. D. (1997). *Bloodlines: From Ethnic Pride to Ethnic Terrorism.* New York: Farrar, Straus and Giroux.

Volkan, V. D. (2004). *Blind Trust: Large Groups and Their Leaders in Times of Crisis and Terror.* Charlottesville, VA: Pitchstone.

Volkan, V. D. (2006). *Killing in the Name of Identity: A Study of Bloody Conflicts.* Charlottesville, VA: Pitchstone.

Volkan, V. D. (2008). On Kemal Atatürk's psychoanalytic biography. In: B. Tezcan & K. K. Babir (Eds.), *Identity and Identity Formation in the Ottoman World: A Volume of Essays in Honor of Norman Itzkowitz.* Madison, WI: University of Wisconsin Press.

Volkan, V. D. (2009). The next chapter: Consequences of societal trauma. In: P. Gobodo-Madikizela & C. van der Merve (Eds.), *Memory, Narrative and Forgiveness: Perspectives of the Unfinished Journeys of the Past* (pp. 1–26). Newcastle upon Tyne, UK: Cambridge Scholars Publishing.

Volkan, V. D. (2011). Play and tract two diplomacy. In: M. C. Akhtar (Ed.), *Play and Playfulness: Developmental, Clinical, and Socio-Cultural Aspects* (pp. 150–171). New York: Jason Aronson.

Volkan, V. D. (2013). *Enemies on the Couch: A Psychopolitical Journey Through War and Peace.* Durham, NC: Pitchstone.

Volkan, V. D. (2017). *Immigrants and Refugees: Trauma, Perennial Mourning, and Border Psychology.* London: Karnac.

Volkan, V. D. (2019). *Ghosts in the Human Psyche: The Story of a 'Muslim Armenian'*. Bicester, Oxfordshire: Phoenix.

Volkan, V. D., & Fowler, J. C. (2009). Large-group narcissism and political leaders with narcissistic personality organization. *Psychiatric Annals, 39*: 214–222.

Volkan, V. D., & Itzkowitz, N. (1984). *The Immortal Atatürk: A Psychobiography*. Chicago, IL: University of Chicago Press.

Volkan, V. D., & Itzkowitz, N. (1994). *Turks and Greeks: Neighbours in Conflict*. Cambridge: Eothen Press.

Volkan, V. D., & Itzkowitz, N. (2011). *Atatürk/Anatürk: Yasamı, İç Dünyası, Yeni Türk Kimliğinin Yaratılması ve Bugünkü Türkiye'de Kimlik Sorunu) (FatherTurk/ MotherTurk: His Life, His Internal World, The Creation of the Modern Turkish Identity and Identity Questions in Today's Turkey)*. Istanbul: Alfa.

Volkan, V. D., Itzkowitz, N., & Dodd, A. (1997). *Richard Nixon: A Psychobiography*. New York: Columbia University Press.

Volkan, V. D., & Zintl, E. (1999). *Life after Loss: The Lessons of Grief*. New York: Charles Scribner's Sons.

Waelder, R. (1936). The principle of multiple function: observations on over-determination. *Psychoanalytic Quarterly, 5*: 45–62.

Werner, H., & Kaplan, B. (1963). *Symbol Formation*. New York: Wiley.

Winnicott, D. W. (1953a). Transitional objects and transitional phenomena. *International Journal of Psychoanalysis, 34*: 89–97.

Winnicott, D. W. (1953b). Transitional phantasies and transitional phenomena: A study of first not-me possession. *International Journal of Psychoanalysis, 34*: 140–152.

Winnicott, C. (1969). Berlin Walls. In: C. Winnicott, R. Sheppard, & M. Davis (Eds.), *D. W. Winnicott: Home is Where We Start From: Essays by a Psychoanalyst* (pp. 221–227). New York: W. W. Norton.

Young, K. (1969). *The Greek Passion: A Study in People and Politics*. London: J. M. Dent and Sons.

Index